Dear Nanilee;
Thanks for
being such a kind
and good help to
Sharri.
Aloha,
Kathy Summers

THE BEST AND EASIEST HANDMADE BREADS

From Start to Finish in 1 and ½ Hours

NUTRITIOUS, ECONOMICAL AND HEALING

THE BEST AND EASIEST HANDMADE BREADS

From Start to Finish in 1 and ½ Hours

NUTRITIOUS, ECONOMICAL AND HEALING

By Kathy Summers

Illustrated by Aloe Corry

Langdon Street Press
212 3rd Avenue North, Suite 290
Minneapolis, MN 55401
612.455.2293
www.langdonstreetpress.com

ISBN - 978-1-934938-63-8
ISBN - 1-934938-63-7
LCCN - 2009939812

Cover Design by Jenni Wheeler
Typeset by James Arneson

Printed in the United States of America

For my dear and courageous Dad who wants to learn to make bread as he deals with painful bone cancer. And for Mom who eats his bread as she takes care of Dad.

For our daughters and their husbands, for our sons and their wives, for our grandchildren; that they may continue to make our bread, for my husband and for God who provides us the ingredients and wisdom to make bread and to share it.

AKNOWLEDGEMENTS

Thanks with all my heart to Rosie Summers, Sylvia McCord, Chris Keith, Rusty Paguiragan, Sarah Corry and Zena Summers for their thoughtful editing.

Special thanks to Aloe Corry, our granddaughter, for doing the illustrations. Aloe is fifteen. This is the first published book she has illustrated.

My gratitude to the people at Mill City Press. I could not have worked with more helpful, excellent people. Special thanks to Michelle Brown, Rosie Cashman, Kim Gaetz and Mark Pitzele.

TABLE OF CONTENTS

INTRODUCTION

Dear friends,

I have made handmade bread almost every day for the last thirty-nine years. We raised a family of nine children and they are mostly made of handmade bread. Being so busy with our children, I had to figure out a way of making bread that was not only nutritious and delicious, but also fast and easy. I have taught our six daughters, many of our grandchildren and hundreds of other people how to make bread. Many say it is the best bread they have ever eaten and the first time they have been successful making bread.

This book takes you carefully through the fundamental knowledge and steps of making bread. All the yeast bread recipes are made with instant yeast. This yeast rises the dough much faster than regular yeast does. The instructions are simple and specific. All you need to do is read and follow each individual recipe. Each recipe has complete instructions. The ingredients are rapidly stirred together. There is a short kneading time and no first rising of the dough. The bread is then shaped, raised, baked and eaten. Every recipe can be completed from start to finish within 1½ hours.

I thought I was done writing bread books. I have written two others, but the enthusiasm I have found from many people still wanting to learn has only increased. Times are hard now. Homemade bread is inexpensive and comfortingly filling.

I have been blessed to create better and easier recipes. Come along and join me in a new book on handmade breads. You'll find old friends and new friends and old ways and new ways to guide your bread-making journey. I hope this is one of the easiest and best bread books you will ever use.

"May the road rise to meet you,
May the wind be always at your back.
May the sun shine warm upon your face,
The rains fall soft upon your fields.
And ...May God hold you in the palm of his hand."

–An Old Irish Blessing

May you be blessed as you make bread for those you love.

Love,

Kathy

GLOSSARY

Boil: to heat a liquid until bubbles rise to the surface and break.

Dough: a dense uncooked mixture of flour, other ingredients, liquid and yeast.

Drizzle: to drip a glaze from the end of a spoon over rolls.

Elasticity: the ability of the dough to stretch and rise.

Fiber: the roughage of the grain.

Fold: to gently lift and turn over the dry ingredients into the wet ingredients until all the dry ingredients have been moistened.

Glaze: to gently paint a liquid topping onto the bread or rolls before they are baked.

Gluten: a part of the wheat berry that contains protein and gives the bread its ability to stretch.

Humidity: the amount of moisture in the air.

Leaven: that which makes the dough or batter rise such as yeast or baking powder.

Rise: the process of the dough growing bigger.

Stir: to combine ingredients with a spoon or whisk using a circular motion.

Yield: the amount a recipe will make.

EQUIPMENT

EQUIPMENT

Take good care of your equipment. Clean it and put it away after you have finished using it. Keep your oven, kitchen counters, tabletop, kitchen cupboards, kitchen drawers and refrigerator clean and organized. Taking care of your tools and your kitchen, makes bread-making an even nicer experience each time you do it.

USEFUL EQUIPMENT TO MAKE BREAD

Apron

Easy-to-clean, flat, smooth, work surface at a comfortable height for stirring and kneading (this can be your kitchen counter or a tabletop)

Small bowl for checking the yeast if that is necessary

Air-tight container for storing the yeast in the refrigerator

Large plastic or metal containers for your bread flour, whole-wheat flour and unbleached-all-purpose flour

Large bowl for stirring the dough

Graduated measuring cups for measuring the liquid and the dry ingredients (1 cup, ½ cup, ⅓ cup, ¼ cup)

Measuring spoons

Oven thermometer to check the temperature of the oven

Large spoon for sifting, measuring, stirring and folding

Small spoon to help measure flour

Dinner knife for leveling the dry ingredients and to help remove the bread from the loaf pans

Straight edged metal spatula to keep the work surface clean and smooth and to lift bread off the baking sheet

Dough scraper can also keep the work surface clean and smooth

Sharp knife for cutting the dough into pieces

Rolling pin to roll out the dough for cinnamon bread and cinnamon rolls

Tape measure or ruler to measure the size of the rolled-out dough

Two 9x5x3-inch non-stick loaf pans

One 16½x11½-inch heavy-duty aluminum baking sheet for rolls, challah bread, French bread, pretzels and breadsticks (use a smaller baking sheet if necessary to fit your oven size)

Spray bottle for spraying the loaf or rolls with water

Soft pastry brush for glazing the bread or rolls

Timer to check the bread's cooking progress at suggested times

Potholders

Wire cooling rack

Cutting board for slicing the bread

Sharp, serrated bread knife for slashing the dough and cutting the bread (take good care of this knife and do not use it for anything else)

Two medium bowls for making muffins

Whisk or fork for beating the liquid ingredients for muffins

Rubber spatula to scrape all the ingredients from the sides of the bowl when making muffins

One 2½-inch standard-size muffin tin

Tin foil muffin liners

Gallon size plastic zipper bags for storing the bread

Paper or cloth bag for storing French bread, pretzels and breadsticks

Gallon size plastic freezer zipper bags for freezing the cooked bread

Permanent marker to write date on yeast container and bread in freezer bags

INGREDIENTS

INGREDIENTS

Most of the ingredients can be purchased from a regular grocery store, but some of the ingredients you will find only at a health food grocery store. Health food grocery stores are now a booming business and are delightful places to shop.

LEAVEN

Leaven is the substance that makes the dough or batter rise.

Yeast, a tiny fungus, is activated by warm water between 110 to 115 degrees. The yeast starts to multiply rapidly. The sweetener feeds the yeast. The bi-product of this activity is carbon dioxide bubbles that get trapped in the stretchy gluten structure of the wheat based bread dough. This is what makes the dough rise.

I use instant yeast in all the yeast recipes. It can be purchased at a kitchen store. This yeast rises much faster than regular yeast. It is packaged in a freeze-dried container that weighs a little more than 1 pound. The package is hard and airtight. When you open it, it turns into granules. Once opened, it must be kept in an airtight container in the refrigerator. The yeast will stay active for 3 months.

The instant yeast can also be purchased in packets. These can be purchased at a grocery store. One packet of yeast contains one tablespoon of yeast. The yeast is more expensive when you buy it in packets rather than in the freeze-dried larger package.

Baking powder makes the muffin batter rise. It is activated first by the liquid ingredients and gives off carbon dioxide bubbles. It reacts a second time when it is heated in the oven.

LIQUIDS

Warm liquid is needed to dissolve and activate the yeast.

Bread made with **water** has a crisp crust, a coarse chewy texture and a pure flavor.

Bread made with **milk** has a velvety grain and an inviting brown crust.

Bread made with **buttermilk** has a fine texture. Buttermilk is skim milk that has bacteria cultures added to thicken it and to give it a sour taste.

WHEAT FLOUR

Wheat flour, which contains gluten, is the fundamental ingredient in any yeast bread. Gluten is the part of the wheat kernel, which stretches around the carbon dioxide bubbles produced by the yeast. Stirring and kneading form the gluten.

Whole-wheat flour, bread flour and unbleached all-purpose flour are all considered wheat flour.

Store all flour in a cool place in airtight containers. If you bake frequently, it is good to store extra bread flour and whole-wheat flour because you will use them the most.

Almost every large grocery store now sells bread flour and whole-wheat flour. Often you can choose between stone-ground and regularly milled flour. Stone ground flour has a coarser texture.

Whole-wheat flour is ground from the entire wheat kernel: the endosperm, the germ and the bran. It has many nutrients and is heavier and more perishable than bread flour or unbleached all-purpose flour.

Wheat germ is high in fiber and nutrition. Wheat germ is removed from whole-wheat to make white flour.

Bread flour is white flour with a high amount of gluten in it. This flour is made from the endosperm of the wheat kernel. The gluten increases the elasticity of the dough and results in bread with higher volume than bread baked with unbleached all-purpose flour.

Unbleached all-purpose flour can be used interchangeably with bread flour. This flour is best to use for muffins. Unbleached all-purpose flour has been refined, but has no added chemicals or preservatives.

Semolina flour is used to make pasta. It is high in protein and is a wonderful addition to French bread, pretzels and breadsticks.

OTHER GRAINS

Oatmeal adds a moist, chewy texture. Oats are high in protein and minerals.

Whole millet is very easy to digest and adds a crunchy texture.

NON-GRAIN FLOUR, FLAKES

Cornmeal is ground from yellow or white corn.

Soy flour is ground from whole soybeans. It adds important protein and fiber.

Flaxseed meal adds fiber and nutrition.

Mashed potato flakes make the bread softer.

SALT

The amount of salt can vary depending on your taste or health needs. Salt controls the growing yeast. Salt enhances the flavor of the bread. I use **iodized salt**. Iodine is a necessary nutrient for a healthy body.

Rock salt has larger particles than regular salt.

SWEETENER

Sweetener provides food for the yeast to grow and also gives flavor and color to the bread. Vary the amount of sweetener to suit your taste or health needs.

Honey is a sweet golden-brown fluid produced by bees from the nectar of flowers.

Maple syrup is syrup made from the sap of the sugar maple tree. It has a wonderful flavor in bread and can be used interchangeably with honey.

Brown sugar is granulated sugar that contains molasses. It is moist and firm.

Granulated sugar is a refined sugar that has all the molasses removed from it.

Molasses is removed from sugar during the refining process. It has a strong, sweet taste.

Powdered sugar is finely ground sugar that has cornstarch added to it to make it easier to blend. It is used in the glaze for cinnamon rolls.

FAT

Fat makes the bread tender, moist and flavorful.

Canola oil is a healthy and inexpensive oil.

Olive oil is a healthy and more expensive oil.

Butter adds wonderful flavor.

Canola cooking spray for spraying the pans.

EGGS

Eggs add tenderness, richness, flavor, color and protein to the bread.

SPICES

Cinnamon

Pumpkin pie spice

EXTRACTS

Vanilla

SEEDS

Fennel

Flax

Poppy

Sesame

Sunflower

CHEESE

Cream cheese

Parmesan cheese

FRESH OR FROZEN FRUIT

Blueberries-fresh or frozen

CANNED VEGETABLE

Pumpkin

DRIED FRUITS

Raisins

Dates

RECIPES

WHITE BREADS AND ROLLS

WHITE BREAD

Excellent for sandwiches and toast. Simple and loved by all.

YIELD

Two 9x5-inch loaves or 12 large or 15 medium rolls

1. CHECK YOUR YEAST

If you store your yeast in an airtight container in the refrigerator, write the expiration date of the yeast on the container with a permanent marker. Use the yeast before the expiration date.

If you are unsure of the expiration date of the yeast, in a small bowl measure 1 cup warm water, 1 tablespoon yeast and 1 tablespoon sugar. Stir until the yeast and sugar dissolve.

Allow the mixture to sit for 10 minutes. If the mixture does not bubble, you must get new yeast before making the bread.

INGREDIENTS YOU WILL NEED FOR WHITE BREAD

2¼ cups warm water
2 tablespoons instant yeast
⅓ cup honey
⅓ cup canola oil
2 level teaspoons salt
5½ to 6½ cups bread flour

Glaze if desired with 1 beaten egg **for loaves** or **for rolls** or 1 tablespoon melted butter **for loaves** or 2 tablespoons melted butter **for rolls**.

2. GETTING READY

As you stay focused on making the bread, your mind will quiet. Enjoy the peacefulness.

Read the entire recipe.

Gather all the equipment and ingredients necessary to make the bread.

Clean a counter space or a tabletop to work on.

For loaves, spray two 9x5-inch non-stick loaf pans with canola cooking spray.

For rolls, spray a 16½x11½-inch heavy-duty aluminum-baking sheet with canola cooking spray.

3. MEASURING AND STIRRING

Use a large spoon for stirring and measuring.

Pour 2¼ cups warm water into a large mixing bowl. Sprinkle 2 tablespoons yeast over the water. Stir until the yeast dissolves.

Add ⅓ cup honey and ⅓ cup canola oil to the yeast mixture. Stir until well blended.

FLOUR

Keep the bread flour in a large metal or plastic container. Before measuring the flour, sift through the flour several times in the flour container with the large spoon. If the flour is packed together, you will get too much flour in each cup.

With the large spoon, scoop the flour into the measuring cup until it is overflowing. This takes about 3 to 4 spoonfuls to do.

With the straight side of a dinner knife, remove the excess flour so that the flour is level with the top of the cup.

Add 2 level teaspoons salt and 3 cups bread flour to the yeast mixture. Stir until mixture is thick and smoothly blended.

Gradually, ½ cup at a time, add about 2½ more cups of bread flour to the mixture. Continue stirring after each addition of flour. This is important in forming the dough. When the dough sticks together and pulls cleanly away from the sides of the bowl, stop adding flour. It may not be necessary to add all the flour.

4. PREHEATING

When you turn the oven on to preheat it, place an oven thermometer in the center of the middle shelf of the oven.

After 20 minutes, read the oven thermometer. You may need to adjust the temperature. Many ovens do not bake at the temperature the dial indicates. Check your oven temperature once every 6 months.

Preheat the oven to 350 degrees. The oven needs to preheat for 20 minutes.

5. KNEADING

Measure 1 more cup bread flour for kneading and shaping.

Lightly flour the work surface. Place the dough on the work surface. Lightly flour the dough.

Fold the dough in half.

Using the heels of your hands, push the dough down and away from you with a rolling motion.

Turn the dough a quarter turn.

Repeat this sequence of folding, pushing and turning for 5 minutes, until the dough is smooth, elastic and easy to handle. The dough will get firmer as you knead.

As you knead, continue to lightly flour the work surface and the dough with flour so the dough does not get sticky.

Knead gently so that you stretch the dough, but do not tear open the smooth surface of the dough.

If dry clumps of flour stick to your hands, wash and dry your hands. Your hands and the work surface should be smooth to knead and shape the dough.

Do not try to mix lumps of dry dough from the bowl or work surface into the dough. They will not blend in.

6. SHAPING

Place the dough to the side and scrape the work surface clean with a metal spatula or dough scraper before shaping.

Take the time to shape the loaves or rolls nicely. Beautiful bread that tastes good is a work of art.

For loaves, lightly flour the work surface and place the dough on the work surface. Lightly flour the dough.

Cut the dough in half.

With the first piece of dough, place the smoothest side face down on the work surface. Next, press the air out of the dough with your hands and form it into a rectangle, approximately 5x4-inches. You are shaping the loaf.

Starting with the 4-inch side nearest you, tightly, but without tearing the outer surface of the dough, roll the dough away from you into a log. Pinch the seam together and push it into the dough. Push in and tuck under the two ends of the dough.

Place the loaf in the loaf pan, seam side down. Adjust the shape so the loaf is symmetrical. It will not fill the entire pan.

Repeat with the second piece of dough. Keep the work surface and the dough lightly floured.

For rolls, lightly flour the work surface and place the dough on the work surface. Lightly flour the dough.

Cut the dough into 12 to 15 equal pieces.

To make rolls, use the smoothest part of the dough as the outside of the roll. Without tearing the outside surface of the dough, stretch and tuck the dough under to form a ball.

Place on the baking sheet.

Repeat with each piece of dough. Leave space between the rolls.

7. RISING

Let the loaves rise until they *almost* double in size. This usually takes about 10 to 15 minutes. Instant yeast raises the dough in half the time of regular yeast.

Let the rolls rise until they double in size. This usually takes about 10 to 15 minutes. Instant yeast raises the dough in half the time of regular yeast.

8. GLAZING (OPTIONAL)

After the bread has risen, the top crust of the bread can be cooked as is or it can be brushed with a beaten egg for a shiny golden crust or it can be brushed with melted butter for a soft crust.

9. BAKING

Place the loaf pans or baking sheet in the center of the middle shelf of the oven.

On the oven shelf, leave space all the way around and between the loaf pans or all the way around the baking sheet to allow the heat to circulate.

Do not open the oven during the first ten minutes of baking because the dough is completing the rising process.

Some ovens are warmer in the back, front, or on one side. Halfway through the baking time, rotate the loaf pans or baking sheet.

Check the loaves and the rolls 5 minutes before the suggested minimal baking time.

Bake the loaves for 25 to 35 minutes or until golden-brown on tops, sides and bottoms. There should be a hollow thump sound when each loaf is tapped on the bottom with your finger. Do not over bake.

Bake the rolls for 15 to 18 minutes or until golden-brown on the tops and bottoms. Do not over bake.

10. COOLING

For loaves, immediately take them out of the pans and place them on a wire cooling rack. Use a dinner knife to run down the sides of the loaf pans, if necessary, to help get the loaves out of the pans. There must be air space around the loaves, including the bottoms, so they do not get wet as they cool.

Cool for 20 minutes before cutting. As the loaves cool, they are actually still cooking and completing the baking process.

When the loaves are cool, slice them on a cutting board with a serrated knife. Use a sawing motion as you cut, so you do not squash the loaves.

For rolls, use a spatula to take the rolls off the baking sheet and place them on a wire cooling rack. There must be air space around the rolls, including the bottoms, so they do not get wet as they cool. Rolls can be eaten warm.

11. THANKING, EATING, SHARING

Give thanks. Eat some. Share some.

12. RECORDING WHAT YOU HAVE LEARNED

Write notes on the recipe about the amount of bread flour you used, the rising time, the baking temperature, the baking time and any changes you may have made to the recipe.

13. STORING

Bread must cool for about 1½ hours before storing it.

Store bread in gallon size plastic zipper bags.

14. FREEZING

Bread that you are not going to eat in the first 2 days should be kept in the freezer.

Store bread in gallon size plastic freezer zipper bags. They are thicker than the regular zipper bags.

Try to get the air out of the bags before closing them.

Write the date on the bags with a permanent marker. Bread can be kept in the freezer for 3 months.

15. DEFROSTING

Defrost the bread by taking it out of the zipper bags.

Brush off any ice crystals.

You can defrost the bread at room temperature on a wire cooling rack.

Sliced bread can be put in a toaster to defrost it.

16. MAKING THIS RECIPE AGAIN

In a couple of days, make this recipe again. Each time it will turn out even better.

POTATO BREAD

Very soft texture. A favorite.

YIELD

Two 9x5-inch loaves or 12 large or 15 medium rolls

1. CHECK YOUR YEAST

If you store your yeast in an airtight container in the refrigerator, write the expiration date of the yeast on the container with a permanent marker. Use the yeast before the expiration date.

If you are unsure of the expiration date of the yeast, in a small bowl measure 1 cup warm water, 1 tablespoon yeast and 1 tablespoon sugar. Stir until the yeast and sugar dissolve.

Allow the mixture to sit for 10 minutes. If the mixture does not bubble, you must get new yeast before making the bread.

INGREDIENTS YOU WILL NEED FOR POTATO BREAD

2¼ cups warm water
2 tablespoons instant yeast
⅓ cup honey
⅓ cup canola oil
2 level teaspoons salt
1 cup mashed potato flakes
4½ to 5½ cups bread flour

Glaze (optional) with 1 beaten egg **for loaves** or **for rolls** or 1 tablespoon melted butter **for loaves** or 2 tablespoons melted butter **for rolls**.

2. GETTING READY

As you stay focused on making the bread, your mind will quiet. Enjoy the peacefulness.

Read the entire recipe.

Gather all the equipment and ingredients necessary to make the bread.

Clean a counter space or a tabletop to work on.

For loaves, spray two 9x5-inch non-stick loaf pans with canola cooking spray.

For rolls, spray a 16½x11½-inch heavy-duty aluminum-baking sheet with canola cooking spray.

3. MEASURING AND STIRRING

Use a large spoon for stirring and measuring.

Pour 2¼ cups warm water into a large mixing bowl. Sprinkle 2 tablespoons yeast over the water. Stir until the yeast dissolves.

Add ⅓ cup honey and ⅓ cup canola oil to the yeast mixture. Stir until well blended.

FLOUR

Keep the bread flour in a large metal or plastic container. Before measuring the flour, sift through the flour several times in the flour container with the large spoon. If the flour is packed together, you will get too much flour in each cup.

With the large spoon, scoop the flour into the measuring cup until it is overflowing. This takes about 3 to 4 spoonfuls to do.

With the straight side of a dinner knife, remove the excess flour so that the flour is level with the top of the cup.

Add 2 level teaspoons salt, 1 cup mashed potato flakes and 2 cups bread flour to the yeast mixture. Stir until mixture is thick and smoothly blended.

Gradually, ½ cup at a time, add about 2½ more cups of bread flour to the mixture. Continue stirring after each addition of flour. This is important in forming the dough. When the dough sticks together and pulls cleanly away from the sides of the bowl, stop adding flour. It may not be necessary to add all the flour.

4. PREHEATING

When you turn the oven on to preheat it, place an oven thermometer in the center of the middle shelf of the oven.

After 20 minutes, read the oven thermometer. You may need to adjust the temperature. Many ovens do not bake at the temperature the dial indicates. Check your oven temperature once every 6 months.

Preheat the oven to 350 degrees. The oven needs to preheat for 20 minutes.

5. KNEADING

Measure 1 more cup bread flour for kneading and shaping.

Lightly flour the work surface. Place the dough on the work surface. Lightly flour the dough.

Fold the dough in half.

Using the heels of your hands, push the dough down and away from you with a rolling motion.

Turn the dough a quarter turn.

Repeat this sequence of folding, pushing and turning for 5 minutes, until the dough is smooth, elastic and easy to handle. The dough will get firmer as you knead.

As you knead, continue to lightly flour the work surface and the dough with flour so the dough does not get sticky.

Knead gently so that you stretch the dough, but do not tear open the smooth surface of the dough.

If dry clumps of flour stick to your hands, wash and dry your hands. Your hands and the work surface should be smooth to knead and shape the dough.

Do not try to mix lumps of dry dough from the bowl or work surface into the dough. They will not blend in.

6. SHAPING

Place the dough to the side and scrape the work surface clean with a metal spatula or dough scraper before shaping.

Take the time to shape the loaves or rolls nicely. Beautiful bread that tastes good is a work of art.

For loaves, lightly flour the work surface and place the dough on the work surface. Lightly flour the dough.

Cut the dough in half.

With the first piece of dough, place the smoothest side face down on the work surface. Next, press the air out of the dough with your hands and form it into a rectangle, approximately 5x4-inches. You are shaping the loaf.

Starting with the 4-inch side nearest you, tightly, but without tearing the outer surface of the dough, roll the dough away from you into a log. Pinch the seam together and push it into the dough. Push in and tuck under the two ends of the dough.

Place the loaf in the loaf pan, seam side down. Adjust the shape so the loaf is symmetrical.

It will not fill the entire pan.

Repeat with the second piece of dough. Keep the work surface and the dough lightly floured.

For rolls, lightly flour the work surface and place the dough on the work surface. Lightly flour the dough.

Cut the dough into 12 to 15 equal pieces.

To make rolls, use the smoothest part of the dough as the outside of the roll. Without tearing the outside surface of the dough, stretch and tuck the dough under to form a ball.

Place on the baking sheet.

Repeat with each piece of dough. Leave space between the rolls.

7. RISING

Let the loaves rise until they *almost* double in size. This usually takes about 10 to 15 minutes. Instant yeast raises the dough in half the time of regular yeast.

Let the rolls rise until they double in size. This usually takes about 10 to 15 minutes. Instant yeast raises the dough in half the time of regular yeast.

8. GLAZING (OPTIONAL)

After the bread has risen, the top crust of the bread can be cooked as is or it can be brushed with a beaten egg for a shiny golden crust or it can be brushed with melted butter for a soft crust.

9. BAKING

Place the loaf pans or baking sheet in the center of the middle shelf of the oven.

On the oven shelf, leave space all the way around and between the loaf pans or all the way around the baking sheet to allow the heat to circulate.

Do not open the oven during the first ten minutes of baking because the dough is completing the rising process.

Some ovens are warmer in the back, front, or on one side. Halfway through the baking time, rotate the loaf pans or baking sheet.

Check the loaves and the rolls 5 minutes before the suggested minimal baking time.

Bake the loaves for 25 to 35 minutes or until golden-brown on tops, sides and bottoms.

There should be a hollow thump sound when each loaf is tapped on the bottom with your finger. Do not over bake.

Bake the rolls for 15 to 18 minutes or until golden-brown on the tops and bottoms. Do not over bake.

10. COOLING

For loaves, immediately take them out of the pans and place them on a wire cooling rack. Use a dinner knife to run down the sides of the loaf pans, if necessary, to help get the loaves out of the pans. There must be air space around the loaves, including the bottoms, so they do not get wet as they cool.

Cool for 20 minutes before cutting. As the loaves cool, they are actually still cooking and completing the baking process.

When the loaves are cool, slice them on a cutting board with a serrated knife. Use a sawing motion as you cut, so you do not squash the loaves.

For rolls, use a spatula to take the rolls off the baking sheet and place them on a wire cooling rack. There must be air space around the rolls, including the bottoms, so they do not get wet as they cool. Rolls can be eaten warm.

11. THANKING, EATING, SHARING

Give thanks. Eat some. Share some.

12. RECORDING WHAT YOU HAVE LEARNED

Write notes on the recipe about the amount of bread flour you used, the rising time, the baking temperature, the baking time and any changes you may have made to the recipe.

13. STORING

Bread must cool for about 1½ hours before storing it.

Store bread in gallon size plastic zipper bags.

14. FREEZING

Bread that you are not going to eat in the first 2 days should be kept in the freezer.

Store bread in gallon size plastic freezer zipper bags. They are thicker than the regular zipper bags.

Try to get the air out of the bags before closing them.

Write the date on the bags with a permanent marker. Bread can be kept in the freezer for 3 months.

15. DEFROSTING

Defrost the bread by taking it out of the zipper bags.

Brush off any ice crystals.

You can defrost the bread at room temperature on a wire cooling rack.

Sliced bread can be put in a toaster to defrost it.

16. MAKING THIS RECIPE AGAIN

In a couple of days, make this recipe again. Each time it will turn out even better.

BUTTERMILK BREAD

Soft and moist. A favorite.

YIELD

Two 9x5-inch loaves or 12 large or 15 medium rolls

1. CHECK YOUR YEAST

If you store your yeast in an airtight container in the refrigerator, write the expiration date of the yeast on the container with a permanent marker. Use the yeast before the expiration date.

If you are unsure of the expiration date of the yeast, in a small bowl measure 1 cup warm water, 1 tablespoon yeast and 1 tablespoon sugar. Stir until the yeast and sugar dissolve.

Allow the mixture to sit for 10 minutes. If the mixture does not bubble, you must get new yeast before making the bread.

INGREDIENTS YOU WILL NEED FOR BUTTERMILK BREAD

1¼ cups warm water
1 cup warm buttermilk
2 tablespoons instant yeast
⅓ cup honey
⅓ cup canola oil
2 level teaspoons salt
5½ to 6½ cups bread flour

Glaze (optional) with 1 beaten egg **for loaves** or **for rolls** or 1 tablespoon melted butter **for loaves** or 2 tablespoons melted butter **for rolls**.

2. GETTING READY

As you stay focused on making the bread, your mind will quiet. Enjoy the peacefulness.

Read the entire recipe.

Gather all the equipment and ingredients necessary to make the bread.

Clean a counter space or a tabletop to work on.

For loaves, spray two 9x5-inch non-stick loaf pans with canola cooking spray.

For rolls, spray a 16½x11½-inch heavy-duty aluminum-baking sheet with canola cooking spray.

3. MEASURING AND STIRRING

Use a large spoon for stirring and measuring.

Pour 1¼ cups warm water and 1 cup warm buttermilk into a large mixing bowl. Sprinkle 2 tablespoons yeast over the liquid. Stir until the yeast dissolves.

Add ⅓ cup honey and ⅓ cup canola oil to the yeast mixture. Stir until well blended.

Flour

Keep the bread flour in a large metal or plastic container. Before measuring the flour, sift through the flour several times in the flour container with the large spoon. If the flour is packed together, you will get too much flour in each cup.

With the large spoon, scoop the flour into the measuring cup until it is overflowing. This takes about 3 to 4 spoonfuls to do.

With the straight side of a dinner knife, remove the excess flour so that the flour is level with the top of the cup.

Add 2 level teaspoons salt and 3 cups bread flour to the yeast mixture. Stir until mixture is thick and smoothly blended.

Gradually, ½ cup at a time, add about 2½ more cups of bread flour to the mixture. Continue stirring after each addition of flour. This is important in forming the dough. When the dough sticks together and pulls cleanly away from the sides of the bowl, stop adding flour. It may not be necessary to add all the flour.

4. PREHEATING

When you turn the oven on to preheat it, place an oven thermometer in the center of the middle shelf of the oven.

After 20 minutes, read the oven thermometer. You may need to adjust the temperature. Many ovens do not bake at the temperature the dial indicates. Check your oven temperature once every 6 months.

Preheat the oven to 350 degrees. The oven needs to preheat for 20 minutes.

5. KNEADING

Measure 1 more cup bread flour for kneading and shaping.

Lightly flour the work surface. Place the dough on the work surface. Lightly flour the dough.

Fold the dough in half.

Using the heels of your hands, push the dough down and away from you with a rolling motion.

Turn the dough a quarter turn.

Repeat this sequence of folding, pushing and turning for 5 minutes, until the dough is smooth, elastic and easy to handle. The dough will get firmer as you knead.

As you knead, continue to lightly flour the work surface and the dough with flour so the dough does not get sticky.

Knead gently so that you stretch the dough, but do not tear open the smooth surface of the dough.

If dry clumps of flour stick to your hands, wash and dry your hands. Your hands and the work surface should be smooth to knead and shape the dough.

Do not try to mix lumps of dry dough from the bowl or work surface into the dough. They will not blend in.

6. SHAPING

Place the dough to the side and scrape the work surface clean with a metal spatula or dough scraper before shaping.

Take the time to shape the loaves or rolls nicely. Beautiful bread that tastes good is a work of art.

For loaves, lightly flour the work surface and place the dough on the work surface. Lightly flour the dough.

Cut the dough in half.

With the first piece of dough, place the smoothest side face down on the work surface. Next, press the air out of the dough with your hands and form it into a rectangle, approximately 5x4-inches. You are shaping the loaf.

Starting with the 4-inch side nearest you, tightly, but without tearing the outer surface of the dough, roll the dough away from you into a log. Pinch the seam together and push it into the dough. Push in and tuck under the two ends of the dough.

Place the loaf in the loaf pan, seam side down. Adjust the shape so the loaf is symmetrical. It will not fill the entire pan.

Repeat with the second piece of dough. Keep the work surface and the dough lightly floured.

For rolls, lightly flour the work surface and place the dough on the work surface. Lightly flour the dough.

Cut the dough into 12 to 15 equal pieces.

To make rolls, use the smoothest part of the dough as the outside of the roll. Without tearing the outside surface of the dough, stretch and tuck the dough under to form a ball.

Place on the baking sheet.

Repeat with each piece of dough. Leave space between the rolls.

7. RISING

Let the loaves rise until they *almost* double in size. This usually takes about 10 to 15 minutes. Instant yeast raises the dough in half the time of regular yeast.

Let the rolls rise until they double in size. This usually takes about 10 to 15 minutes. Instant yeast raises the dough in half the time of regular yeast.

8. GLAZING (OPTIONAL)

Cook the top crust as is or brush with a beaten egg for a shiny golden crust or brush with butter for a soft crust.

9. BAKING

Place the loaf pans or baking sheet in the center of the middle shelf of the oven.

On the oven shelf, leave space all the way around and between the loaf pans or all the way around the baking sheet to allow the heat to circulate.

Do not open the oven during the first ten minutes of baking because the dough is completing the rising process.

Some ovens are warmer in the back, front, or on one side. Halfway through the baking time, rotate the loaf pans or baking sheet.

Check the loaves and the rolls 5 minutes before the suggested minimal baking time.

Bake the loaves for 25 to 35 minutes or until golden-brown on tops, sides and bottoms. There should be a hollow thump sound when each loaf is tapped on the bottom with your finger. Do not over bake.

Bake the rolls for 15 to 18 minutes or until golden-brown on the tops and bottoms. Do not over bake.

10. COOLING

For loaves, immediately take them out of the pans and place them on a wire cooling rack. Use a dinner knife to run down the sides of the loaf pans, if necessary, to help get the loaves out of the pans. There must be air space around the loaves, including the bottoms, so they do not get wet as they cool.

Cool for 20 minutes before cutting. As the loaves cool, they are actually still cooking and completing the baking process.

When the loaves are cool, slice them on a cutting board with a serrated knife. Use a sawing motion as you cut, so you do not squash the loaves.

For rolls, use a spatula to take the rolls off the baking sheet and place them on a wire cooling rack. There must be air space around the rolls, including the bottoms, so they do not get wet as they cool. Rolls can be eaten warm.

11. THANKING, EATING, SHARING

Give thanks. Eat some. Share some.

12. RECORDING WHAT YOU HAVE LEARNED

Write notes on the recipe about the amount of bread flour you used, the rising time, the baking temperature, the baking time and any changes you may have made to the recipe.

13. STORING

Bread must cool for about 1½ hours before storing it. Store bread in gallon size plastic zipper bags.

14. FREEZING

Bread that you are not going to eat in the first 2 days should be kept in the freezer.

Store bread in gallon size plastic freezer zipper bags. They are thicker than the regular zipper bags.

Try to get the air out of the bags before closing them.

Write the date on the bags with a permanent marker. Bread can be kept in the freezer for 3 months.

15. DEFROSTING

Defrost the bread by taking it out of the zipper bags.

Brush off any ice crystals.

You can defrost the bread at room temperature on a wire cooling rack.

Sliced bread can be put in a toaster to defrost it.

16. MAKING THIS RECIPE AGAIN

In a couple of days, make this recipe again. Each time it will turn out even better.

NUTRITIOUS WHITE BREAD

High protein, wonderful taste.

YIELD

Two 9x5-inch loaves or 12 large or 15 medium rolls

1. CHECK YOUR YEAST

If you store your yeast in an airtight container in the refrigerator, write the expiration date of the yeast on the container with a permanent marker. Use the yeast before the expiration date.

If you are unsure of the expiration date of the yeast, in a small bowl measure 1 cup warm water, 1 tablespoon yeast and 1 tablespoon sugar. Stir until the yeast and sugar dissolve.

Allow the mixture to sit for 10 minutes. If the mixture does not bubble, you must get new yeast before making the bread.

INGREDIENTS YOU WILL NEED FOR NUTRITIOUS WHITE BREAD

2 cups warm water
2 tablespoons instant yeast
⅓ cup pure maple syrup
⅓ cup olive oil
I egg
2 level teaspoons salt
½ cup dry milk powder
½ cup wheat germ
½ cup soy flour
4½ to 5½ cups bread flour

Glaze (optional) with 1 beaten egg **for loaves** or **for rolls** or 1 tablespoon melted butter **for loaves** or 2 tablespoons melted butter **for rolls**.

2. GETTING READY

As you stay focused on making the bread, your mind will quiet. Enjoy the peacefulness.

Read the entire recipe.

Gather all the equipment and ingredients necessary to make the bread.

Clean a counter space or a tabletop to work on.

For loaves, spray two 9x5-inch non-stick loaf pans with canola cooking spray.

For rolls, spray a 16½x11½-inch heavy-duty aluminum-baking sheet with canola cooking spray.

3. MEASURING AND STIRRING

Use a large spoon for stirring and measuring.

Pour 2 cups warm water into a large mixing bowl. Sprinkle 2 tablespoons yeast over the water. Stir until the yeast dissolves.

Add ⅓ pure maple syrup, ⅓ cup olive oil and 1 egg to the yeast mixture. Stir until well blended.

Flour

Keep the bread flour in a large metal or plastic container. Before measuring the flour, sift through the flour several times in the flour container with the large spoon. If the flour is packed together, you will get too much flour in each cup.

With the large spoon, scoop the flour into the measuring cup until it is overflowing. This takes about 3 to 4 spoonfuls to do.

With the straight side of a dinner knife, remove the excess flour so that the flour is level with the top of the cup.

Spoon the wheat germ and the soy flour into the measuring cup, using a smaller spoon.

Add 2 level teaspoons salt, ½ cup dry milk powder, ½ cup wheat germ, ½ cup soy flour and 2 cups bread flour to the yeast mixture. Stir until mixture is thick and smoothly blended.

Gradually, ½ cup at a time, add about 2½ more cups of bread flour to the mixture. Continue stirring after each addition of flour. This is important in forming the dough. When the dough sticks together and pulls cleanly away from the sides of the bowl, stop adding flour. It may not be necessary to add all the flour.

4. PREHEATING

When you turn the oven on to preheat it, place an oven thermometer in the center of the middle shelf of the oven.

After 20 minutes, read the oven thermometer. You may need to adjust the temperature. Many ovens do not bake at the temperature the dial indicates. Check your oven temperature once every 6 months.

Preheat the oven to 350 degrees. The oven needs to preheat for 20 minutes.

5. KNEADING

Measure 1 more cup bread flour for kneading and shaping.

Lightly flour the work surface. Place the dough on the work surface. Lightly flour the dough.

Fold the dough in half.

Using the heels of your hands, push the dough down and away from you with a rolling motion.

Turn the dough a quarter turn.

Repeat this sequence of folding, pushing and turning for 5 minutes, until the dough is smooth, elastic and easy to handle. The dough will get firmer as you knead.

As you knead, continue to lightly flour the work surface and the dough with flour so the dough does not get sticky.

Knead gently so that you stretch the dough, but do not tear open the smooth surface of the dough.

If dry clumps of flour stick to your hands, wash and dry your hands. Your hands and the work surface should be smooth to knead and shape the dough.

Do not try to mix lumps of dry dough from the bowl or work surface into the dough. They will not blend in.

6. SHAPING

Place the dough to the side and scrape the work surface clean with a metal spatula or dough scraper before shaping.

Take the time to shape the loaves or rolls nicely. Beautiful bread that tastes good is a work of art.

For loaves, lightly flour the work surface and place the dough on the work surface. Lightly flour the dough.

Cut the dough in half.

With the first piece of dough, place the smoothest side face down on the work surface. Next, press the air out of the dough with your hands and form it into a rectangle, approximately 5x4-inches. You are shaping the loaf.

Starting with the 4-inch side nearest you, tightly, but without tearing the outer surface of the dough, roll the dough away from you into a log. Pinch the seam together and push it into the dough. Push in and tuck under the two ends of the dough.

Place the loaf in the loaf pan, seam side down. Adjust the shape so the loaf is symmetrical. It will not fill the entire pan.

Repeat with the second piece of dough. Keep the work surface and the dough lightly floured.

For rolls, lightly flour the work surface and place the dough on the work surface. Lightly flour the dough.

Cut the dough into 12 to 15 equal pieces.

To make rolls, use the smoothest part of the dough as the outside of the roll. Without tearing the outside surface of the dough, stretch and tuck the dough under to form a ball.

Place on the baking sheet.

Repeat with each piece of dough. Leave space between the rolls.

7. RISING

Let the loaves rise until they *almost* double in size. This usually takes about 10 to 15 minutes. Instant yeast raises the dough in half the time of regular yeast.

Let the rolls rise until they double in size. This usually takes about 10 to 15 minutes. Instant yeast raises the dough in half the time of regular yeast.

8. GLAZING (OPTIONAL)

Cook the top crust as is or brush with a beaten egg for a shiny golden crust or brush with butter for a soft crust.

9. BAKING

Place the loaf pans or baking sheet in the center of the middle shelf of the oven.
On the oven shelf, leave space all the way around and between the loaf pans or all the way around the baking sheet to allow the heat to circulate.

Do not open the oven during the first ten minutes of baking because the dough is completing the rising process.

Some ovens are warmer in the back, front, or on one side. Halfway through the baking time, rotate the loaf pans or baking sheet.

Check the loaves and the rolls 5 minutes before the suggested minimal baking time.

Bake the loaves for 25 to 35 minutes or until golden-brown on tops, sides and bottoms. There should be a hollow thump sound when each loaf is tapped on the bottom with your finger. Do not over bake.

Bake the rolls for 15 to 18 minutes or until golden-brown on the tops and bottoms. Do not over bake.

10. COOLING

For loaves, immediately take them out of the pans and place them on a wire cooling rack. Use a dinner knife to run down the sides of the loaf pans, if necessary, to help get the loaves out of the pans. There must be air space around the loaves, including the bottoms, so they do not get wet as they cool.

Cool for 20 minutes before cutting. As the loaves cool, they are actually still cooking and completing the baking process.

When the loaves are cool, slice them on a cutting board with a serrated knife. Use a sawing motion as you cut, so you do not squash the loaves.

For rolls, use a spatula to take the rolls off the baking sheet and place them on a wire cooling rack. There must be air space around the rolls, including the bottoms, so they do not get wet as they cool. Rolls can be eaten warm.

11. THANKING, EATING, SHARING

Give thanks. Eat some. Share some.

12. RECORDING WHAT YOU HAVE LEARNED

Write notes on the recipe about the amount of bread flour you used, the rising time, the baking temperature, the baking time and any changes you may have made to the recipe.

13. STORING

Bread must cool for about 1½ hours before storing it.

Store bread in gallon size plastic zipper bags.

14. FREEZING

Bread that you are not going to eat in the first 2 days should be kept in the freezer.

Store bread in gallon size plastic freezer zipper bags. They are thicker than the regular zipper bags.

Try to get the air out of the bags before closing them.

Write the date on the bags with a permanent marker. Bread can be kept in the freezer for 3 months.

15. DEFROSTING

Defrost the bread by taking it out of the zipper bags.

Brush off any ice crystals.

You can defrost the bread at room temperature on a wire cooling rack.

Sliced bread can be put in a toaster to defrost it.

16. MAKING THIS RECIPE AGAIN

In a couple of days, make this recipe again. Each time it will turn out even better.

WHOLE GRAIN BREADS AND ROLLS

WHOLE-WHEAT BREAD

Great for sandwiches and toast. Kids love this bread. Mild wheat flavor.

YIELD

Two 9x5-inch loaves or 12 large or 15 medium rolls

1. CHECK YOUR YEAST

If you store your yeast in an airtight container in the refrigerator, write the expiration date of the yeast on the container with a permanent marker. Use the yeast before the expiration date.

If you are unsure of the expiration date of the yeast, in a small bowl measure 1 cup warm water, 1 tablespoon yeast and 1 tablespoon sugar. Stir until the yeast and sugar dissolve.

Allow the mixture to sit for 10 minutes. If the mixture does not bubble, you must get new yeast before making the bread.

INGREDIENTS YOU WILL NEED FOR WHOLE-WHEAT BREAD

2¼ cups warm water
2 tablespoons instant yeast
⅓ cup honey
⅓ cup canola oil
2 level teaspoons salt
3¼ cups whole-wheat flour
2 to 3 cups bread flour

Glaze (optional) with 1 beaten egg **for loaves** or **for rolls** or 1 tablespoon melted butter **for loaves** or 2 tablespoons melted butter **for rolls**.

2. GETTING READY

As you stay focused on making the bread, your mind will quiet. Enjoy the peacefulness.

Read the entire recipe.

Gather all the equipment and ingredients necessary to make the bread.

Clean a counter space or a tabletop to work on.

For loaves, spray two 9x5-inch non-stick loaf pans with canola cooking spray.

For rolls, spray a 16½x11½-inch heavy-duty aluminum-baking sheet with canola cooking spray.

3. MEASURING AND STIRRING

Use a large spoon for stirring and measuring.

Pour 2¼ cups warm water into a large mixing bowl. Sprinkle 2 tablespoons yeast over the water. Stir until the yeast dissolves.

Add ⅓ cup honey and ⅓ cup canola oil to the yeast mixture. Stir until well blended.

Flour

Keep the whole-wheat flour and bread flour in large metal or plastic containers. Before measuring the flour, sift through the flour several times in the flour container with the large spoon. If the flour is packed together, you will get too much flour in each cup.

With the large spoon, scoop the flour into the measuring cup until it is overflowing. This takes about 3 to 4 spoonfuls to do.

With the straight side of a dinner knife, remove the excess flour so that the flour is level with the top of the cup.

Add 2 level teaspoons salt and 3¼ cups whole-wheat flour to the yeast mixture. Stir until mixture is thick and smoothly blended.

Gradually, ½ cup at a time, add about 2 more cups of bread flour to the mixture. Continue stirring after each addition of flour. This is important in forming the dough. When the dough sticks together and pulls cleanly away from the sides of the bowl, stop adding flour.

4. PREHEATING

When you turn the oven on to preheat it, place an oven thermometer in the center of the middle shelf of the oven.

After 20 minutes, read the oven thermometer. You may need to adjust the temperature. Many ovens do not bake at the temperature the dial indicates. Check your oven temperature once every 6 months.

Preheat the oven to 350 degrees. The oven needs to preheat for 20 minutes.

5. KNEADING

Measure 1 more cup bread flour for kneading and shaping.

Lightly flour the work surface. Place the dough on the work surface. Lightly flour the dough.

Fold the dough in half.

Using the heels of your hands, push the dough down and away from you with a rolling motion.

Turn the dough a quarter turn.

Repeat this sequence of folding, pushing and turning for 5 minutes, until the dough is smooth, elastic and easy to handle. The dough will get firmer as you knead.

As you knead, continue to lightly flour the work surface and the dough with flour so the dough does not get sticky.

Knead gently so that you stretch the dough, but do not tear open the smooth surface of the dough.

If dry clumps of flour stick to your hands, wash and dry your hands. Your hands and the work surface should be smooth to knead and shape the dough.

Do not try to mix lumps of dry dough from the bowl or work surface into the dough. They will not blend in.

6. SHAPING

Place the dough to the side and scrape the work surface clean with a metal spatula or dough scraper before shaping.

Take the time to shape the loaves or rolls nicely. Beautiful bread that tastes good is a work of art.

For loaves, lightly flour the work surface and place the dough on the work surface. Lightly flour the dough.

Cut the dough in half.

With the first piece of dough, place the smoothest side face down on the work surface. Next, press the air out of the dough with your hands and form it into a rectangle, approximately 5x4-inches. You are shaping the loaf.

Starting with the 4-inch side nearest you, tightly, but without tearing the outer surface of the dough, roll the dough away from you into a log. Pinch the seam together and push it into the dough. Push in and tuck under the two ends of the dough.

Place the loaf in the loaf pan, seam side down. Adjust the shape so the loaf is symmetrical. It will not fill the entire pan.

Repeat with the second piece of dough. Keep the work surface and the dough lightly floured.

For rolls, lightly flour the work surface and place the dough on the work surface. Lightly flour the dough.

Cut the dough into 12 to 15 equal pieces.

To make rolls, use the smoothest part of the dough as the outside of the roll. Without tearing the outside surface of the dough, stretch and tuck the dough under to form a ball.

Place on the baking sheet.

Repeat with each piece of dough. Leave space between the rolls.

7. RISING

Let the loaves rise until they *almost* double in size. This usually takes about 10 to 15 minutes. Instant yeast raises the dough in half the time of regular yeast.

Let the rolls rise until they double in size. This usually takes about 10 to 15 minutes. Instant yeast raises the dough in half the time of regular yeast.

8. GLAZING (OPTIONAL)

Cook the top crust as is or brush with a beaten egg for a shiny golden crust or brush with butter for a soft crust.

9. BAKING

Place the loaf pans or baking sheet in the center of the middle shelf of the oven.

On the oven shelf, leave space all the way around and between the loaf pans or all the way around the baking sheet to allow the heat to circulate.

Do not open the oven during the first ten minutes of baking because the dough is completing the rising process.

Some ovens are warmer in the back, front, or on one side. Halfway through the baking time, rotate the loaf pans or baking sheet.

Check the loaves and the rolls 5 minutes before the suggested minimal baking time.

Bake the loaves for 25 to 35 minutes or until golden-brown on tops, sides and bottoms. There should be a hollow thump sound when each loaf is tapped on the bottom with your finger. Do not over bake.

Bake the rolls for 15 to 18 minutes or until golden-brown on the tops and bottoms. Do not over bake.

10. COOLING

For loaves, immediately take them out of the pans and place them on a wire cooling rack. Use a dinner knife to run down the sides of the loaf pans, if necessary, to help get the loaves out of the pans. There must be air space around the loaves, including the bottoms, so they do not get wet as they cool.

Cool for 20 minutes before cutting. As the loaves cool, they are actually still cooking and completing the baking process.

When the loaves are cool, slice them on a cutting board with a serrated knife. Use a sawing motion as you cut, so you do not squash the loaves.

For rolls, use a spatula to take the rolls off the baking sheet and place them on a wire cooling rack. There must be air space around the rolls, including the bottoms, so they do not get wet as they cool. Rolls can be eaten warm.

11. THANKING, EATING, SHARING

Give thanks. Eat some. Share some.

12. RECORDING WHAT YOU HAVE LEARNED

Write notes on the recipe about the amount of bread flour you used, the rising time, the baking temperature, the baking time and any changes you may have made to the recipe.

13. STORING

Bread must cool for about 1½ hours before storing it.

Store bread in gallon size plastic zipper bags.

14. FREEZING

Bread that you are not going to eat in the first 2 days should be kept in the freezer.

Store bread in gallon size plastic freezer zipper bags. They are thicker than the regular zipper bags.

Try to get the air out of the bags before closing them.

Write the date on the bags with a permanent marker. Bread can be kept in the freezer for 3 months.

15. DEFROSTING

Defrost the bread by taking it out of the zipper bags.

Brush off any ice crystals.

You can defrost the bread at room temperature on a wire cooling rack.

Sliced bread can be put in a toaster to defrost it.

16. MAKING THIS RECIPE AGAIN

In a couple of days, make this recipe again. Each time it will turn out even better.

100% WHOLE-WHEAT BREAD

Hearty and healthy.

YIELD

Two 9x5-inch loaves or 12 large or 15 medium rolls

1. CHECK YOUR YEAST

If you store your yeast in an airtight container in the refrigerator, write the expiration date of the yeast on the container with a permanent marker. Use the yeast before the expiration date.

If you are unsure of the expiration date of the yeast, in a small bowl measure 1 cup warm water, 1 tablespoon yeast and 1 tablespoon sugar. Stir until the yeast and sugar dissolve.

Allow the mixture to sit for 10 minutes. If the mixture does not bubble, you must get new yeast before making the bread.

INGREDIENTS YOU WILL NEED FOR 100% WHOLE-WHEAT BREAD

2¼ cups warm water
2 tablespoons instant yeast
⅓ cup honey
⅓ cup canola oil
2 level teaspoons salt
5¼ to 6¼ cups whole-wheat flour

Glaze (optional) with 1 beaten egg **for loaves** or **for rolls** or 1 tablespoon melted butter **for loaves** or 2 tablespoons melted butter **for rolls**.

2. GETTING READY

As you stay focused on making the bread, your mind will quiet. Enjoy the peacefulness.

Read the entire recipe.

Gather all the equipment and ingredients necessary to make the bread.

Clean a counter space or a tabletop to work on.

For loaves, spray two 9x5-inch non-stick loaf pans with canola cooking spray.

For rolls, spray a 16½x11½-inch heavy-duty aluminum-baking sheet with canola cooking spray.

3. MEASURING AND STIRRING

Use a large spoon for stirring and measuring.

Pour 2¼ cups warm water into a large mixing bowl. Sprinkle 2 tablespoons yeast over the water. Stir until the yeast dissolves.

Add ⅓ cup honey and ⅓ cup canola oil to the yeast mixture. Stir until well blended.

Flour

Keep the whole-wheat flour in a large metal or plastic container. Before measuring the flour, sift through the flour several times in the flour container with the large spoon. If the flour is packed together, you will get too much flour in each cup.

With the large spoon, scoop the flour into the measuring cup until it is overflowing. This takes about 3 to 4 spoonfuls to do.

With the straight side of a dinner knife, remove the excess flour so that the flour is level with the top of the cup.

Add 2 level teaspoons of salt and 3¼ cups whole-wheat flour to the yeast mixture. Stir until mixture is thick and smoothly blended.

Gradually, ½ cup at a time, add about 2 more cups of whole-wheat flour to the mixture. Continue stirring after each addition of flour. This is important in forming the dough. When the dough sticks together and pulls cleanly away from the sides of the bowl, stop adding flour.

4. PREHEATING

When you turn the oven on to preheat it, place an oven thermometer in the center of the middle shelf of the oven.

After 20 minutes, read the oven thermometer. You may need to adjust the temperature. Many ovens do not bake at the temperature the dial indicates. Check your oven temperature once every 6 months.

Preheat the oven to 350 degrees. The oven needs to preheat for 20 minutes.

5. KNEADING

Measure 1 more cup whole-wheat flour for kneading and shaping.

Lightly flour the work surface. Place the dough on the work surface. Lightly flour the dough.

Fold the dough in half.

Using the heels of your hands, push the dough down and away from you with a rolling motion.

Turn the dough a quarter turn.

Repeat this sequence of folding, pushing and turning for 5 minutes, until the dough is smooth, elastic and easy to handle. The dough will get firmer as you knead.

As you knead, continue to lightly flour the work surface and the dough with flour so the dough does not get sticky.

Knead gently so that you stretch the dough, but do not tear open the smooth surface of the dough.

If dry clumps of flour stick to your hands, wash and dry your hands. Your hands and the work surface should be smooth to knead and shape the dough.

Do not try to mix lumps of dry dough from the bowl or work surface into the dough. They will not blend in.

6. SHAPING

Place the dough to the side and scrape the work surface clean with a metal spatula or dough scraper before shaping.

Take the time to shape the loaves or rolls nicely. Beautiful bread that tastes good is a work of art.

For loaves, lightly flour the work surface and place the dough on the work surface. Lightly flour the dough.

Cut the dough in half.

With the first piece of dough, place the smoothest side face down on the work surface. Next, press the air out of the dough with your hands and form it into a rectangle, approximately 5x4-inches. You are shaping the loaf.

Starting with the 4-inch side nearest you, tightly, but without tearing the outer surface of the dough, roll the dough away from you into a log. Pinch the seam together and push it into the dough. Push in and tuck under the two ends of the dough.

Place the loaf in the loaf pan, seam side down. Adjust the shape so the loaf is symmetrical. It will not fill the entire pan.

Repeat with the second piece of dough. Keep the work surface and the dough lightly floured.

For rolls, lightly flour the work surface and place the dough on the work surface. Lightly flour the dough.

Cut the dough into 12 to 15 equal pieces.

To make rolls, use the smoothest part of the dough as the outside of the roll. Without tearing the outside surface of the dough, stretch and tuck the dough under to form a ball.

Place on the baking sheet.

Repeat with each piece of dough. Leave space between the rolls.

7. RISING

Let the loaves rise until they *almost* double in size. This usually takes about 10 to 15 minutes. Instant yeast raises the dough in half the time of regular yeast.

Let the rolls rise until they double in size. This usually takes about 10 to 15 minutes. Instant yeast raises the dough in half the time of regular yeast.

8. GLAZING (OPTIONAL)

Cook the top crust as is or brush with a beaten egg for a shiny golden crust or brush with butter for a soft crust.

9. BAKING

Place the loaf pans or baking sheet in the center of the middle shelf of the oven. On the oven shelf, leave space all the way around and between the loaf pans or all the way around the baking sheet to allow the heat to circulate.

Do not open the oven during the first ten minutes of baking because the dough is completing the rising process.

Some ovens are warmer in the back, front, or on one side. Halfway through the baking time, rotate the loaf pans or baking sheet.

Check the loaves and the rolls 5 minutes before the suggested minimal baking time.

Bake the loaves for 25 to 35 minutes or until golden-brown on tops, sides and bottoms. There should be a hollow thump sound when each loaf is tapped on the bottom with your finger. Do not over bake.

Bake the rolls for 15 to 18 minutes or until golden-brown on the tops and bottoms. Do not over bake.

10. COOLING

For loaves, immediately take them out of the pans and place them on a wire cooling rack. Use a dinner knife to run down the sides of the loaf pans, if necessary, to help get the loaves out of the pans. There must be air space around the loaves, including the bottoms, so they do not get wet as they cool.

Cool for 20 minutes before cutting. As the loaves cool, they are actually still cooking and completing the baking process.

When the loaves are cool, slice them on a cutting board with a serrated knife. Use a sawing motion as you cut, so you do not squash the loaves.

For rolls, use a spatula to take the rolls off the baking sheet and place them on a wire cooling rack. There must be air space around the rolls, including the bottoms, so they do not get wet as they cool. Rolls can be eaten warm.

11. THANKING, EATING, SHARING

Give thanks. Eat some. Share some.

12. RECORDING WHAT YOU HAVE LEARNED

Write notes on the recipe about the amount of whole-wheat flour you used, the rising time, the baking temperature, the baking time and any changes you may have made to the recipe.

13. STORING

Bread must cool for about 1½ hours before storing it.

Store bread in gallon size plastic zipper bags.

14. FREEZING

Bread that you are not going to eat in the first 2 days should be kept in the freezer.

Store bread in gallon size plastic freezer zipper bags. They are thicker than the regular zipper bags.

Try to get the air out of the bags before closing them.

Write the date on the bags with a permanent marker. Bread can be kept in the freezer for 3 months.

15. DEFROSTING

Defrost the bread by taking it out of the zipper bags.

Brush off any ice crystals.

You can defrost the bread at room temperature on a wire cooling rack.

Sliced bread can be put in a toaster to defrost it.

16. MAKING THIS RECIPE AGAIN

In a couple of days, make this recipe again. Each time it will turn out even better.

MUTLI-GRAIN BREAD

A hearty bread that combines the flavors of several grains.

YIELD

Two 9x5-inch loaves or 12 large or 15 medium rolls

1. CHECK YOUR YEAST

If you store your yeast in an airtight container in the refrigerator, write the expiration date of the yeast on the container with a permanent marker. Use the yeast before the expiration date.

If you are unsure of the expiration date of the yeast, in a small bowl measure 1 cup warm water, 1 tablespoon yeast and 1 tablespoon sugar. Stir until the yeast and sugar dissolve.

Allow the mixture to sit for 10 minutes. If the mixture does not bubble, you must get new yeast before making the bread.

INGREDIENTS YOU WILL NEED FOR MUTLI-GRAIN BREAD

2¼ cups warm water
2 tablespoons instant yeast
⅓ cup honey
1 tablespoon molasses
⅓ cup olive oil
2 level teaspoons salt
¼ cup flaxseed meal
¼ cup wheat germ
¼ cup corn meal
¼ soy flour
1 cup whole-wheat flour
3½ to 4½ cups bread flour

Glaze (optional) with 1 beaten egg **for loaves** or **for rolls** or 1 tablespoon melted butter **for loaves** or 2 tablespoons melted butter **for rolls**.

2. GETTING READY

As you stay focused on making the bread, your mind will quiet. Enjoy the peacefulness.

Read the entire recipe.

Gather all the equipment and ingredients necessary to make the bread.

Clean a counter space or a tabletop to work on.

For loaves, spray two 9x5-inch non-stick loaf pans with canola cooking spray.

For rolls, spray a 16½x11½-inch heavy-duty aluminum-baking sheet with canola cooking spray.

3. MEASURING AND STIRRING

Use a large spoon for stirring and measuring.

Pour 2¼ cups warm water into a large mixing bowl. Sprinkle 2 tablespoons yeast over the water. Stir until the yeast dissolves.

Add ⅓ cup honey, 1 tablespoon molasses and ⅓ cup olive oil to the yeast mixture. Stir until well blended.

Flour

Keep the whole-wheat flour and bread flour in large metal or plastic containers. Before measuring the flour, sift through the flour several times in the flour container with the large spoon. If the flour is packed together, you will get too much flour in each cup.

With the large spoon, scoop the flour into the measuring cup until it is overflowing. This takes about 3 to 4 spoonfuls to do.

Then with the straight side of a dinner knife, remove the excess flour so that the flour is level with the top of the cup.

Spoon the flaxseed meal, wheat germ, corn meal and soy flour into the measuring cup, using a smaller spoon.

Add 2 level teaspoons salt, ¼ cup flaxseed meal, ¼ cup wheat germ, ¼ cup corn meal, ¼ soy flour, 1 cup whole-wheat flour and 1 cup bread flour to the yeast mixture. Stir until mixture is thick and smoothly blended.

Gradually, ½ cup at a time, add about 2½ more cups of bread flour to the mixture. Continue stirring after each addition of flour. This is important in forming the dough. When the dough sticks together and pulls cleanly away from the sides of the bowl, stop adding flour. It may not be necessary to add all the flour.

4. PREHEATING

When you turn the oven on to preheat it, place an oven thermometer in the center of the middle shelf of the oven.

After 20 minutes, read the oven thermometer. You may need to adjust the temperature. Many ovens do not bake at the temperature the dial indicates. Check your oven temperature once every 6 months.

Preheat the oven to 350 degrees. The oven needs to preheat for 20 minutes.

5. KNEADING

Measure 1 more cup bread flour for kneading and shaping.

Lightly flour the work surface. Place the dough on the work surface. Lightly flour the dough.

Fold the dough in half.

Using the heels of your hands, push the dough down and away from you with a rolling motion.

Turn the dough a quarter turn.

Repeat this sequence of folding, pushing and turning for 5 minutes, until the dough is smooth, elastic and easy to handle. The dough will get firmer as you knead.

As you knead, continue to lightly flour the work surface and the dough with flour so the dough does not get sticky.

Knead gently so that you stretch the dough, but do not tear open the smooth surface of the dough.

If dry clumps of flour stick to your hands, wash and dry your hands. Your hands and the work surface should be smooth to knead and shape the dough.

Do not try to mix lumps of dry dough from the bowl or work surface into the dough. They will not blend in.

6. SHAPING

Place the dough to the side and scrape the work surface clean with a metal spatula or dough scraper before shaping.

Take the time to shape the loaves or rolls nicely. Beautiful bread that tastes good is a work of art.

For loaves, lightly flour the work surface and place the dough on the work surface. Lightly flour the dough.

Cut the dough in half.

With the first piece of dough, place the smoothest side face down on the work surface. Next, press the air out of the dough with your hands and form it into a rectangle, approximately 5x4-inches. You are shaping the loaf.

Starting with the 4-inch side nearest you, tightly, but without tearing the outer surface of the dough, roll the dough away from you into a log. Pinch the seam together and push it into the dough. Push in and tuck under the two ends of the dough.

Place the loaf in the loaf pan, seam side down. Adjust the shape so the loaf is symmetrical. It will not fill the entire pan.

Repeat with the second piece of dough. Keep the work surface and the dough lightly floured.

For rolls, lightly flour the work surface and place the dough on the work surface. Lightly flour the dough.

Cut the dough into 12 to 15 equal pieces.

To make rolls, use the smoothest part of the dough as the outside of the roll. Without tearing the outside surface of the dough, stretch and tuck the dough under to form a ball.

Place on the baking sheet.

Repeat with each piece of dough. Leave space between the rolls.

7. RISING

Let the loaves rise until they *almost* double in size. This usually takes about 10 to 15 minutes. Instant yeast raises the dough in half the time of regular yeast.

Let the rolls rise until they double in size. This usually takes about 10 to 15 minutes. Instant yeast raises the dough in half the time of regular yeast.

8. GLAZING (OPTIONAL)

Cook the top crust as is or brush with a beaten egg for a shiny golden crust or brush with butter for a soft crust.

9. BAKING

Place the loaf pans or baking sheet in the center of the middle shelf of the oven.

On the oven shelf, leave space all the way around and between the loaf pans or all the way around the baking sheet to allow the heat to circulate.

Do not open the oven during the first ten minutes of baking because the dough is completing the rising process.

Some ovens are warmer in the back, front, or on one side. Halfway through the baking time, rotate the loaf pans or baking sheet.

Check the loaves and the rolls 5 minutes before the suggested minimal baking time.

Bake the loaves for 25 to 35 minutes or until golden-brown on tops, sides and bottoms.

There should be a hollow thump sound when each loaf is tapped on the bottom with your finger. Do not over bake.

Bake the rolls for 15 to 18 minutes or until golden-brown on the tops and bottoms. Do not over bake.

10. COOLING

For loaves, immediately take them out of the pans and place them on a wire cooling rack. Use a dinner knife to run down the sides of the loaf pans, if necessary, to help get the loaves out of the pans. There must be air space around the loaves, including the bottoms, so they do not get wet as they cool.

Cool for 20 minutes before cutting. As the loaves cool, they are actually still cooking and completing the baking process.

When the loaves are cool, slice them on a cutting board with a serrated knife. Use a sawing motion as you cut, so you do not squash the loaves.

For rolls, use a spatula to take the rolls off the baking sheet and place them on a wire cooling rack. There must be air space around the rolls, including the bottoms, so they do not get wet as they cool. Rolls can be eaten warm.

11. THANKING, EATING, SHARING

Give thanks. Eat some. Share some.

12. RECORDING WHAT YOU HAVE LEARNED

Write notes on the recipe about the amount of bread flour you used, the rising time, the baking temperature, the baking time and any changes you may have made to the recipe.

13. STORING

Bread must cool for about 1½ hours before storing it.

Store bread in gallon size plastic zipper bags.

14. FREEZING

Bread that you are not going to eat in the first 2 days should be kept in the freezer.

Store bread in gallon size plastic freezer zipper bags. They are thicker than the regular zipper bags.

Try to get the air out of the bags before closing them.

Write the date on the bags with a permanent marker. Bread can be kept in the freezer for 3 months.

15. DEFROSTING

Defrost the bread by taking it out of the zipper bags.

Brush off any ice crystals.

You can defrost the bread at room temperature on a wire cooling rack.

Sliced bread can be put in a toaster to defrost it.

16. MAKING THIS RECIPE AGAIN

In a couple of days, make this recipe again. Each time it will turn out even better.

SEED BREAD

A dense, nutritious bread, filled with fiber.

YIELD

Two 9x5-inch loaves or 12 large rolls or 15 medium rolls

1. CHECK YOUR YEAST

If you store your yeast in an airtight container in the refrigerator, write the expiration date of the yeast on the container with a permanent marker. Use the yeast before the expiration date.

If you are unsure of the expiration date of the yeast, in a small bowl measure 1 cup warm water, 1 tablespoon yeast and 1 tablespoon sugar. Stir until the yeast and sugar dissolve.

Allow the mixture to sit for 10 minutes. If the mixture does not bubble, you must get new yeast before making the bread.

INGREDIENTS YOU WILL NEED FOR SEED BREAD

2¼ cups warm water
2 tablespoons instant yeast
⅓ cup honey
⅓ cup olive oil
2 level teaspoons salt
3¼ cups whole-wheat flour
1 tablespoon flaxseeds
1 tablespoon fennel seeds
1 tablespoon sesame seeds
1 tablespoon whole millet
½ cup sunflower seeds
2 to 3 cups bread flour

Glaze (optional) with 1 beaten egg **for loaves** or **for rolls** or 1 tablespoon melted butter **for loaves** or 2 tablespoons melted butter **for rolls**.

2. GETTING READY

As you stay focused on making the bread, your mind will quiet. Enjoy the peacefulness.

Read the entire recipe.

Gather all the equipment and ingredients necessary to make the bread.

Clean a counter space or a tabletop to work on.

For loaves, spray two 9x5-inch non-stick loaf pans with canola cooking spray.

For rolls, spray a 16½x11½-inch heavy-duty aluminum-baking sheet with canola cooking spray.

3. MEASURING AND STIRRING

Use a large spoon for stirring and measuring.

Pour 2¼ cups warm water into a large mixing bowl. Sprinkle 2 tablespoons yeast over the water. Stir until the yeast dissolves.

Add ⅓ cup honey and ⅓ cup olive oil to the yeast mixture. Stir until well blended.

Flour

Keep the whole-wheat flour and bread flour in large metal or plastic containers. Before measuring the flour, sift through the flour several times in the flour container with the large spoon. If the flour is packed together, you will get too much flour in each cup.

With the large spoon, scoop the flour into the measuring cup until it is overflowing. This takes about 3 to 4 spoonfuls to do.

With the straight side of a dinner knife, remove the excess flour so that the flour is level with the top of the cup.

Add 2 level teaspoons salt, 3¼ cups whole-wheat flour, 1 tablespoon flaxseeds, 1 tablespoon fennel seeds, 1 tablespoon sesame seeds, 1 tablespoon whole millet and ½ cup sunflower seeds to the yeast mixture. Stir until mixture is thick and smoothly blended.

Gradually, ½ cup at a time, add about 2 cups of bread flour to the mixture. Continue stirring after each addition of flour. This is important in forming the dough. When the dough sticks together and pulls cleanly away from the sides of the bowl, stop adding flour.

4. PREHEATING

When you turn the oven on to preheat it, place an oven thermometer in the center of the middle shelf of the oven.

After 20 minutes, read the oven thermometer. You may need to adjust the temperature. Many ovens do not bake at the temperature the dial indicates. Check your oven temperature once every 6 months.

Preheat the oven to 350 degrees. The oven needs to preheat for 20 minutes.

5. KNEADING

Measure 1 more cup bread flour for kneading and shaping.

Lightly flour the work surface. Place the dough on the work surface. Lightly flour the dough.

Fold the dough in half.

Using the heels of your hands, push the dough down and away from you with a rolling motion.

Turn the dough a quarter turn.

Repeat this sequence of folding, pushing and turning for 5 minutes, until the dough is smooth, elastic and easy to handle. The dough will get firmer as you knead.

As you knead, continue to lightly flour the work surface and the dough with flour so the dough does not get sticky.

Knead gently so that you stretch the dough, but do not tear open the smooth surface of the dough.

If dry clumps of flour stick to your hands, wash and dry your hands. Your hands and the work surface should be smooth to knead and shape the dough.

Do not try to mix lumps of dry dough from the bowl or work surface into the dough. They will not blend in.

6. SHAPING

Place the dough to the side and scrape the work surface clean with a metal spatula or dough scraper before shaping.

Take the time to shape the loaves or rolls nicely. Beautiful bread that tastes good is a work of art.

For loaves, lightly flour the work surface and place the dough on the work surface. Lightly flour the dough.

Cut the dough in half.

With the first piece of dough, place the smoothest side face down on the work surface. Next, press the air out of the dough with your hands and form it into a rectangle, approximately 5x4-inches. You are shaping the loaf.

Starting with the 4-inch side nearest you, tightly, but without tearing the outer surface of the dough, roll the dough away from you into a log. Pinch the seam together and push it into the dough. Push in and tuck under the two ends of the dough.

Place the loaf in the loaf pan, seam side down. Adjust the shape so the loaf is symmetrical. It will not fill the entire pan.

Repeat with the second piece of dough. Keep the work surface and the dough lightly floured.

For rolls, lightly flour the work surface and place the dough on the work surface. Lightly flour the dough.

Cut the dough into 12 to 15 equal pieces.

To make rolls, use the smoothest part of the dough as the outside of the roll. Without tearing the outside surface of the dough, stretch and tuck the dough under to form a ball.

Place on the baking sheet.

Repeat with each piece of dough. Leave space between the rolls.

7. RISING

Let the loaves rise until they *almost* double in size. This usually takes about 10 to 15 minutes. Instant yeast raises the dough in half the time of regular yeast.

Let the rolls rise until they double in size. This usually takes about 10 to 15 minutes. Instant yeast raises the dough in half the time of regular yeast.

8. GLAZING (OPTIONAL)

Cook the top crust as is or brush with a beaten egg for a shiny golden crust or brush with butter for a soft crust.

9. BAKING

Place the loaf pans or baking sheet in the center of the middle shelf of the oven.

On the oven shelf, leave space all the way around and between the loaf pans or all the way around the baking sheet to allow the heat to circulate.

Do not open the oven during the first ten minutes of baking because the dough is completing the rising process.

Some ovens are warmer in the back, front, or on one side. Halfway through the baking time, rotate the loaf pans or baking sheet.

Check the loaves and the rolls 5 minutes before the suggested minimal baking time.

Bake the loaves for 25 to 35 minutes or until golden-brown on tops, sides and bottoms.

There should be a hollow thump sound when each loaf is tapped on the bottom with your finger. Do not over bake.

Bake the rolls for 15 to 18 minutes or until golden-brown on the tops and bottoms. Do not over bake.

10. COOLING

For loaves, immediately take them out of the pans and place them on a wire cooling rack. Use a dinner knife to run down the sides of the loaf pans, if necessary, to help get the loaves out of the pans. There must be air space around the loaves, including the bottoms, so they do not get wet as they cool.

Cool for 20 minutes before cutting. As the loaves cool, they are actually still cooking and completing the baking process.

When the loaves are cool, slice them on a cutting board with a serrated knife. Use a sawing motion as you cut, so you do not squash the loaves.

For rolls, use a spatula to take the rolls off the baking sheet and place them on a wire cooling rack. There must be air space around the rolls, including the bottoms, so they do not get wet as they cool. Rolls can be eaten warm.

11. THANKING, EATING, SHARING

Give thanks. Eat some. Share some.

12. RECORDING WHAT YOU HAVE LEARNED

Write notes on the recipe about the amount of bread flour you used, the rising time, the baking temperature, the baking time and any changes you may have made to the recipe.

13. STORING

Bread must cool for about 1½ hours before storing it.

Store bread in gallon size plastic zipper bags.

14. FREEZING

Bread that you are not going to eat in the first 2 days should be kept in the freezer.

Store bread in gallon size plastic freezer zipper bags. They are thicker than the regular zipper bags.

Try to get the air out of the bags before closing them.

Write the date on the bags with a permanent marker. Bread can be kept in the freezer for 3 months.

15. DEFROSTING

Defrost the bread by taking it out of the zipper bags.

Brush off any ice crystals.

You can defrost the bread at room temperature on a wire cooling rack.

Sliced bread can be put in a toaster to defrost it.

16. MAKING THIS RECIPE AGAIN

In a couple of days, make this recipe again. Each time it will turn out even better.

OATMEAL RAISIN BREAD

Nourishing and comforting.

YIELD

Two 9x5-inch loaves or 12 large or 15 medium rolls

1. CHECK YOUR YEAST

If you store your yeast in an airtight container in the refrigerator, write the expiration date of the yeast on the container with a permanent marker. Use the yeast before the expiration date.

If you are unsure of the expiration date of the yeast, in a small bowl measure 1 cup warm water, 1 tablespoon yeast and 1 tablespoon sugar. Stir until the yeast and sugar dissolve.

Allow the mixture to sit for 10 minutes. If the mixture does not bubble, you must get new yeast before making the bread.

INGREDIENTS YOU WILL NEED FOR OATMEAL RAISIN BREAD

1¼ cups warm water
1 cup warm milk
2 tablespoons instant yeast
⅓ cup pure maple syrup
⅓ cup canola oil
2 level teaspoons salt
1 teaspoon cinnamon
1 cup whole oats
1½ cups whole-wheat flour
3 to 4 cups bread flour
1 cup soft raisins

Glaze (optional) with 1 beaten egg **for loaves** or **for rolls** or 1 tablespoon melted butter **for loaves** or 2 tablespoons melted butter **for rolls**.

2. GETTING READY

As you stay focused on making the bread, your mind will quiet. Enjoy the peacefulness.

Read the entire recipe.

Gather all the equipment and ingredients necessary to make the bread.

Clean a counter space or a tabletop to work on.

For loaves, spray two 9x5-inch non-stick loaf pans with canola cooking spray.

For rolls, spray a 16½x11½-inch heavy-duty aluminum-baking sheet with canola cooking spray.

3. MEASURING AND STIRRING

Use a large spoon for stirring and measuring.

Pour 1¼ cups warm water and 1 cup warm milk into a large mixing bowl. Sprinkle 2 tablespoons yeast over the liquid. Stir until the yeast dissolves.

Add ⅓ cup pure maple syrup and ⅓ cup canola oil to the yeast mixture. Stir until well blended.

Flour

Keep the whole-wheat flour and the bread flour in large metal or plastic containers. Before measuring the flour, sift through the flour several times in the flour container with the large spoon. If the flour is packed together, you will get too much flour in each cup.

With the large spoon, scoop the flour into the measuring cup until it is overflowing. This takes about 3 to 4 spoonfuls to do.

With the straight side of a dinner knife, remove the excess flour so that the flour is level with the top of the cup.

Add 2 level teaspoons salt, 1 teaspoon cinnamon, I cup whole oats, 1½ cup whole-wheat flour, 1 cup bread flour and 1 cup soft raisins to the yeast mixture. Stir until mixture is thick and smoothly blended.

Gradually, ½ cup at a time, add about 2 more cups of bread flour to the mixture. Continue stirring after each addition of flour. This is important in forming the dough. When the dough sticks together and pulls cleanly away from the sides of the bowl, stop adding flour.

4. PREHEATING

When you turn the oven on to preheat it, place an oven thermometer in the center of the middle shelf of the oven.

After 20 minutes, read the oven thermometer. You may need to adjust the temperature.

Many ovens do not bake at the temperature the dial indicates. Check your oven temperature once every 6 months.

Preheat the oven to 350 degrees. The oven needs to preheat for 20 minutes.

5. KNEADING

Measure 1 more cup bread flour for kneading and shaping.

Lightly flour the work surface. Place the dough on the work surface. Lightly flour the dough.

Fold the dough in half.

Using the heels of your hands, push the dough down and away from you with a rolling motion.

Turn the dough a quarter turn.

Repeat this sequence of folding, pushing and turning for 5 minutes, until the dough is smooth, elastic and easy to handle. The dough will get firmer as you knead.

As you knead, continue to lightly flour the work surface and the dough with flour so the dough does not get sticky.

Knead gently so that you stretch the dough, but do not tear open the smooth surface of the dough.

If dry clumps of flour stick to your hands, wash and dry your hands. Your hands and the work surface should be smooth to knead and shape the dough.

Do not try to mix lumps of dry dough from the bowl or work surface into the dough. They will not blend in.

6. SHAPING

Place the dough to the side and scrape the work surface clean with a metal spatula or dough scraper before shaping.

Take the time to shape the loaves or rolls nicely. Beautiful bread that tastes good is a work of art.

For loaves, lightly flour the work surface and place the dough on the work surface. Lightly flour the dough.

Cut the dough in half.

With the first piece of dough, place the smoothest side face down on the work surface.

Next, press the air out of the dough with your hands and form it into a rectangle, approximately 5x4-inches. You are shaping the loaf.

Starting with the 4-inch side nearest you, tightly, but without tearing the outer surface of the dough, roll the dough away from you into a log. Pinch the seam together and push it into the dough. Push in and tuck under the two ends of the dough.

Place the loaf in the loaf pan, seam side down. Adjust the shape so the loaf is symmetrical. It will not fill the entire pan.

Repeat with the second piece of dough. Keep the work surface and the dough lightly floured.

For rolls, lightly flour the work surface and place the dough on the work surface. Lightly flour the dough.

Cut the dough into 12 to 15 equal pieces.

To make rolls, use the smoothest part of the dough as the outside of the roll. Without tearing the outside surface of the dough, stretch and tuck the dough under to form a ball.

Place on the baking sheet.

Repeat with each piece of dough. Leave space between the rolls.

7. RISING

Let the loaves rise until they *almost* double in size. This usually takes about 10 to 15 minutes. Instant yeast raises the dough in half the time of regular yeast.

Let the rolls rise until they double in size. This usually takes about 10 to 15 minutes. Instant yeast raises the dough in half the time of regular yeast.

8. GLAZING (OPTIONAL)

Cook the top crust as is or brush with a beaten egg for a shiny golden crust or brush with butter for a soft crust.

9. BAKING

Place the loaf pans or baking sheet in the center of the middle shelf of the oven.

On the oven shelf, leave space all the way around and between the loaf pans or all the way around the baking sheet to allow the heat to circulate.

Do not open the oven during the first ten minutes of baking because the dough is completing the rising process.

Some ovens are warmer in the back, front, or on one side. Halfway through the baking time, rotate the loaf pans or baking sheet.

Check the loaves and the rolls 5 minutes before the suggested minimal baking time.

Bake the loaves for 25 to 35 minutes or until golden-brown on tops, sides and bottoms.

There should be a hollow thump sound when each loaf is tapped on the bottom with your finger. Do not over bake.

Bake the rolls for 15 to 18 minutes or until golden-brown on the tops and bottoms. Do not over bake.

10. COOLING

For loaves, immediately take them out of the pans and place them on a wire cooling rack. Use a dinner knife to run down the sides of the loaf pans, if necessary, to help get the loaves out of the pans. There must be air space around the loaves, including the bottoms, so they do not get wet as they cool.

Cool for 20 minutes before cutting. As the loaves cool, they are actually still cooking and completing the baking process.

When the loaves are cool, slice them on a cutting board with a serrated knife. Use a sawing motion as you cut, so you do not squash the loaves.

For rolls, use a spatula to take the rolls off the baking sheet and place them on a wire cooling rack. There must be air space around the rolls, including the bottoms, so they do not get wet as they cool. Rolls can be eaten warm.

11. THANKING, EATING, SHARING

Give thanks. Eat some. Share some.

12. RECORDING WHAT YOU HAVE LEARNED

Write notes on the recipe about the amount of bread flour you used, the rising time, the baking temperature, the baking time and any changes you may have made to the recipe.

13. STORING

Bread must cool for about 1½ hours before storing it.

Store bread in gallon size plastic zipper bags.

14. FREEZING

Bread that you are not going to eat in the first 2 days should be kept in the freezer.

Store bread in gallon size plastic freezer zipper bags. They are thicker than the regular zipper bags.

Try to get the air out of the bags before closing them.

Write the date on the bags with a permanent marker. Bread can be kept in the freezer for 3 months.

15. DEFROSTING

Defrost the bread by taking it out of the zipper bags.

Brush off any ice crystals.

You can defrost the bread at room temperature on a wire cooling rack.

Sliced bread can be put in a toaster to defrost it.

16. MAKING THIS RECIPE AGAIN

In a couple of days, make this recipe again. Each time it will turn out even better.

SWEET BREADS AND ROLLS

CHALLAH BREAD

Challah is a beautiful braided bread of Jewish origin.
The eggs, honey and oil make it almost cake-like.

YIELD

1 large braided loaf

1. CHECK YOUR YEAST

If you store your yeast in an airtight container in the refrigerator, write the expiration date of the yeast on the container with a permanent marker. Use the yeast before the expiration date.

If you are unsure of the expiration date of the yeast, in a small bowl measure 1 cup warm water, 1 tablespoon yeast and 1 tablespoon sugar. Stir until the yeast and sugar dissolve.

Allow the mixture to sit for 10 minutes. If the mixture does not bubble, you must get new yeast before making the bread.

INGREDIENTS YOU WILL NEED FOR CHALLAH BREAD

1 cup warm water
2 tablespoons instant yeast
⅓ cup brown sugar
⅓ cup canola oil
2 large eggs
1 level teaspoon salt
3½ cups to 4½ cups bread flour

Glaze

1 beaten egg

Topping

1 tablespoon sesame seeds or 1 tablespoon poppy seeds

2. GETTING READY

As you stay focused on making the bread, your mind will quiet. Enjoy the peacefulness.

Read the entire recipe.

Gather all the equipment and ingredients necessary to make the bread.

Clean a counter space or a tabletop to work on.

Spray a 16½x11½-inch heavy-duty aluminum-baking sheet with canola cooking spray.

3. MEASURING AND STIRRING

Use a large spoon for stirring and measuring.

Pour 1 cup warm water into a large mixing bowl. Sprinkle 2 tablespoons instant yeast over the water. Stir until the yeast dissolves.

Add ⅓ cup brown sugar, ⅓ cup canola oil and 2 large eggs to the yeast mixture. Stir until well blended.

FLOUR

Keep the bread flour in a large metal or plastic container. Before measuring the flour, sift through the flour several times in the flour container with a large spoon. If the flour is packed together, you will get too much flour in each cup.

Use a large spoon to scoop the flour into the measuring cup, until it is overflowing. This takes about 3 to 4 spoonfuls to do.

With the straight side of a dinner knife, remove the excess flour so that the flour is level with the top of the cup.

Add 1 level teaspoon salt and 2½ cups bread flour to the yeast mixture. Stir until mixture is thick and smoothly blended.

Gradually, ¼ cup at a time, add about 1 more cup of bread flour to the mixture. Continue stirring after each addition of flour. This is important in forming the dough. When the dough sticks together and pulls cleanly away from the sides of the bowl, stop adding flour.

4. PREHEATING

When you turn the oven on to preheat it, place an oven thermometer in the center of the middle shelf of the oven.

After 20 minutes, read the oven thermometer. You may need to adjust the temperature. Many ovens do not bake at the temperature the dial indicates. Check your oven temperature once every 6 months.

Preheat the oven to 350 degrees. The oven needs to preheat for 20 minutes.

5. KNEADING

Measure 1 more cup bread flour for kneading and shaping.

Lightly flour the work surface. Place the dough on the work surface. Lightly flour the dough.

Fold the dough in half.

Using the heels of your hands, push the dough down and away from you with a rolling motion.

Turn the dough a quarter turn.

Repeat this sequence of folding, pushing and turning for 5 minutes, until the dough is smooth, elastic and easy to handle. The dough will get firmer as you knead.

As you knead, continue to lightly flour the work surface and the dough with flour so the dough does not get sticky.

Knead gently so that you stretch the dough, but do not tear open the smooth surface of the dough.

If dry clumps of flour stick to your hands, wash and dry your hands. Your hands and the work surface should be smooth to knead and shape the dough.

Do not try to mix lumps of dry dough from the bowl or work surface into the dough. They will not blend in.

6. SHAPING

Place the dough to the side and scrape the work surface clean with a metal spatula or dough scraper before shaping.

Take the time to shape the loaf nicely. Beautiful bread that tastes good is a work of art.

Lightly flour the work surface and place the dough on the work surface and lightly flour the dough.

Cut the dough into 3 equal pieces.

Shape each piece into a ball by using the smoothest part of the dough as the outside of the ball. Without tearing the outside surface of the dough, stretch and tuck the dough under to form a ball.

Let the balls rest on the work surface for 3 minutes, so they will be easier to work with as you form the loaf.

Keep the work surface and the dough lightly floured.

Place the smooth side of the ball face down on the work surface. Roll into a 15-inch long rope. Do the same with the other two balls.

Next, loosely braid the ropes.

Pinch each end of the dough together and tuck under. Place the loaf on the baking sheet.

7. RISING

Let the loaf rise until *almost* double in size, a process that usually takes about 15 to 20 minutes.

8. GLAZING

Brush the top crust of the loaf with a beaten egg.

9. TOPPING

Sprinkle with 1 tablespoon sesame seeds or sprinkle with 1 tablespoon poppy seeds.

10. BAKING

Place the baking sheet in the center of the middle shelf of the oven.

On the oven shelf leave space all the way around the baking sheet to allow the heat to circulate.

Do not open the oven during the first 10 minutes of baking because the dough is completing the rising process.

Some ovens are warmer in the back, front or on one side. Halfway through the baking time, rotate the baking sheet.

Check the loaf 5 minutes before the suggested minimal baking time.

Bake the loaf for 35 to 40 minutes or until golden-brown on the top, sides and bottom. Do not over bake.

11. COOLING

When the loaf has finished baking, immediately take it off the baking sheet and place it on a wire cooling rack. There must be air space around the loaf, including the bottom, so it does not get wet as it cools.

Cool for 20 minutes before cutting. As the loaf cools, it is actually still cooking and completing the baking process.

When the loaf is cool, slice it on a cutting board with a serrated knife. Use a sawing motion as you cut, so you do not squash the loaf.

12. THANKING, EATING, SHARING

Give thanks. Eat some. Share some.

13. RECORDING WHAT YOU HAVE LEARNED

Write notes on the recipe about the amount of bread flour you used, the rising time, the baking temperature, the baking time and any changes you may have made to the recipe.

14. STORING

The loaf must cool for about 1½ hours before storing it.

Store bread in gallon size plastic zipper bags.

15. FREEZING

Bread that you are not going to eat in the first 2 days should be kept in the freezer.

Store bread in gallon size plastic freezer zipper bags. They are thicker than the regular zipper bags.

Try to get the air out of the bags before closing them.

Write the date on the bags with a permanent marker. Bread can be kept in the freezer for 3 months.

16. DEFROSTING

Defrost the bread by taking it out of the zipper bags.

Brush off any ice crystals.

You can defrost the bread at room temperature on a wire cooling rack.

Sliced bread can be put in a toaster to defrost it.

17. MAKING THIS RECIPE AGAIN

In a couple of days, make this recipe again. Each time it will turn out even better.

CINNAMON BREAD

Our kids love this cinnamon bread. We use brown sugar instead of white sugar in the cinnamon mixture. People say it is the best cinnamon bread they have ever tasted.

YIELD

Two 9x5-inch loaves

1. CHECK YOUR YEAST

If you store your yeast in an airtight container in the refrigerator, write the expiration date of the yeast on the container with a permanent marker. Use the yeast before the expiration date.

If you are unsure of the expiration date of the yeast, in a small bowl measure 1 cup warm water, 1 tablespoon yeast and 1 tablespoon sugar. Stir until the yeast and sugar dissolve.

Allow the mixture to sit for 10 minutes. If the mixture does not bubble, you must get new yeast before making the bread.

INGREDIENTS YOU WILL NEED FOR CINNAMON BREAD

1 cup warm water
1 cup warm milk
2 tablespoons instant yeast
⅓ cup honey
⅓ cup canola oil
1 egg
2 level teaspoons salt
½ cup whole-wheat flour
1 cup mashed potato flakes
4 to 5 cups bread flour

Filling

2 tablespoons melted butter
1 cup brown sugar
4 teaspoons cinnamon

2. GETTING READY

As you stay focused on making the bread, your mind will quiet. Enjoy the peacefulness.

Read the entire recipe.

Gather all the equipment and ingredients necessary to make the bread.

Clean a counter space or a tabletop to work on.

Spray two 9x5-inch non-stick loaf pans with canola cooking spray.

3. MEASURING AND STIRRING

Use a large spoon for stirring and measuring.

Pour 1 cup warm water and 1 cup warm milk into a large mixing bowl. Sprinkle 2 tablespoons yeast over the liquid. Stir until the yeast dissolves.

Add ⅓ cup honey, ⅓ cup canola oil and 1 egg to the yeast mixture. Stir until well blended.

Flour

Keep the whole-wheat flour and bread flour in large metal or plastic containers. Before measuring the flour, sift through the flour several times in the flour container with the large spoon. If the flour is packed together, you will get too much flour in each cup.

With the large spoon, scoop the flour into the measuring cup until it is overflowing. This takes about 3 to 4 spoonfuls to do.

With the straight side of a dinner knife, remove the excess flour so that the flour is level with the top of the cup.

Add 2 level teaspoons of salt, ½ cup whole-wheat flour, 1 cup mashed potato flakes and 2 cups bread flour bread flour to the yeast mixture. Stir until mixture is thick and smoothly blended.

Gradually, ½ cup at a time, add about 2 more cups of bread flour to the mixture. Continue stirring after each addition of flour. This is important in forming the dough. When the dough sticks together and pulls cleanly away from the sides of the bowl, stop adding flour. It may not be necessary to add all the flour.

4. PREHEATING

When you turn the oven on to preheat it, place an oven thermometer in the center of the middle shelf of the oven.

After 20 minutes, read the oven thermometer. You may need to adjust the temperature. Many ovens do not bake at the temperature the dial indicates. Check your oven temperature once every 6 months.

Preheat the oven to 350 degrees. The oven needs to preheat for 20 minutes.

5. KNEADING

Measure 1 more cup bread flour for kneading and shaping.

Lightly flour the work surface. Place the dough on the work surface. Lightly flour the dough.

Fold the dough in half.

Using the heels of your hands, push the dough down and away from you with a rolling motion.

Turn the dough a quarter turn.

Repeat this sequence of folding, pushing and turning for 5 minutes, until the dough is smooth, elastic and easy to handle. The dough will get firmer as you knead.

As you knead, continue to lightly flour the work surface and the dough with flour so the dough does not get sticky.

Knead gently so that you stretch the dough, but do not tear open the smooth surface of the dough.

If dry clumps of flour stick to your hands, wash and dry your hands. Your hands and the work surface should be smooth to knead and shape the dough.

Do not try to mix lumps of dry dough from the bowl or work surface into the dough. They will not blend in.

6. SHAPING

Place the dough to the side and scrape the work surface clean with a metal spatula or dough scraper before shaping.

Take the time to shape the loaves nicely. Beautiful bread that tastes good is a work of art.

Lightly flour the work surface and place the dough on the work surface. Lightly flour the dough.

Cut the dough in half.

Form each half into a ball. Use the smoothest part of the dough as the outside of the ball. Without tearing the outside surface of the dough, stretch and tuck the dough under to form a ball.

Let the balls rest on the work surface for 3 minutes.

Keep the work surface and the dough lightly floured.

Using your hand and a rolling pin, pat and roll the first ball out into a 15x9-inch rectangle. The exact size does not matter.

Filling

Melt 2 tablespoons butter.

Brush the dough lightly with 1 tablespoon melted butter. Leave a ½ inch border all the way around the dough without butter.

In a small bowl, mix 1 cup brown sugar with 4 teaspoons cinnamon.

Sprinkle the buttered area of the dough with ½ of the cinnamon mixture. Spread it out evenly with your hand.

Starting with the 9-inch side nearest you, firmly roll the dough away from you into a log. You are shaping the loaf. Pinch the seam together and push into the dough. Push in and tuck under the two ends of the dough.

Place the loaf in the loaf pan, seam side down. Adjust the shape so the loaf is symmetrical. It will not fill the entire pan.

Repeat with the second ball.

7. RISING

Let the loaves rise until they *almost* double in size. Usually this takes about 10 to 15 minutes. The instant yeast raises the dough in half the time of regular yeast.

8. BAKING

Place the loaf pans in the center of the middle shelf of the oven.

On the oven shelf, leave space all the way around and between the loaf pans to allow the heat to circulate.

Do not open the oven during the first 10 minutes of baking because the dough is completing the rising process.

Some ovens are warmer in the back, front or on one side. Halfway through the baking time, rotate the loaf pans.

Check the loaves 5 minutes before the suggested minimal baking time.

Bake the loaves for 25 to 35 minutes or until golden-brown on the top, sides and bottom. There should be a hollow thump sound when each loaf is tapped on the bottom with your finger. Do not over bake.

9. COOLING

When the loaves have finished baking, immediately take them out of the pans and place them on a wire cooling rack. Use a dinner knife to run down the sides of the loaf pans, if necessary, to help get the loaves out of the pans. There must be air space around the loaves, including the bottoms, so they do not get wet as they cool.

Cool for 20 minutes before cutting. As the loaves cool, they are actually still cooking and completing the baking process.

When the loaves are cool, slice them on a cutting board with a serrated knife. Use a sawing motion as you cut, so you do not squash the loaves.

10. THANKING, EATING, SHARING

Give thanks. Eat some. Share some.

11. RECORDING WHAT YOU HAVE LEARNED

Write notes on the recipe about the amount of bread flour you used, the rising time, the baking temperature, the baking time and any changes you may have made to the recipe.

12. STORING

Bread must cool for about 1½ hours before storing it.

Store bread in gallon size plastic zipper bags.

13. FREEZING

Bread that you are not going to eat in the first 2 days should be kept in the freezer.

Store bread in gallon size plastic freezer zipper bags. They are thicker than the regular zipper bags.

Try to get the air out of the bags before closing them.

Write the date on the bags with a permanent marker. Bread can be kept in the freezer for 3 months.

14. DEFROSTING

Defrost the bread by taking it out of the zipper bags.

Brush off any ice crystals.

You can defrost the bread at room temperature on a wire cooling rack.

Sliced bread can be put in a toaster to defrost it.

15. MAKING THIS RECIPE AGAIN

In a couple of days, make this recipe again. Each time it will turn out even better.

CINNAMON/RAISIN BREAD

Sprinkle the buttered area of the dough with ½ of the cinnamon mixture. Spread it out evenly with your hand.

Sprinkle ½ cup soft raisins on the cinnamon mixture before you roll up the dough.

Repeat with the second loaf.

CINNAMON ROLLS

Soft, sweet, delicious.

YIELD

12 rolls

1. CHECK YOUR YEAST

If you store your yeast in an airtight container in the refrigerator, write the expiration date of the yeast on the container with a permanent marker. Use the yeast before the expiration date.

If you are unsure of the expiration date of the yeast, in a small bowl measure 1 cup warm water, 1 tablespoon yeast and 1 tablespoon sugar. Stir until the yeast and sugar dissolve.

Allow the mixture to sit for 10 minutes. If the mixture does not bubble, you must get new yeast before making the bread.

INGREDIENTS YOU WILL NEED FOR CINNAMON ROLLS

½ cup warm water
½ cup warm buttermilk
1 tablespoon instant yeast
¼ cup honey
¼ cup cool melted butter
2 eggs
1 level teaspoon salt
½ cup potato flakes
3 to 4 cups bread flour

Filling

1 tablespoon melted butter
½ cup granulated sugar
1½ teaspoons of cinnamon

Glaze

¾ cup powdered sugar
1 tablespoon melted butter

1 tablespoon soft cream cheese
1 teaspoon vanilla flavoring
1 to 2 tablespoons milk

2. GETTING READY

As you stay focused on making the bread, your mind will quiet. Enjoy the peacefulness.

Read the entire recipe.

Gather all the equipment and ingredients necessary to make the bread.

Clean a counter space or a tabletop to work

Spray a 16½x11½-inch heavy-duty aluminum-baking sheet with canola cooking spray.

3. MEASURING AND STIRRING

Use a large spoon for stirring and measuring.

Pour ½ cup warm water and ½ cup warm buttermilk into a large mixing bowl. Sprinkle 1 tablespoon yeast over the liquid. Stir until the yeast dissolves.

Add ¼ cup honey, ¼ cup cool melted butter and 2 eggs to the yeast mixture. Stir until well blended.

Flour

Keep the bread flour in a large metal or plastic container. Before measuring the flour, sift through the flour several times in the flour container with the large spoon. If the flour is packed together, you will get too much flour in each cup.

With the large spoon, scoop the flour into the measuring cup until it is overflowing. This takes about 3 to 4 spoonfuls to do.

With the straight side of a dinner knife, remove the excess flour so that the flour is level with the top of the cup.

Add 1 level teaspoon salt, ½ cup potato flakes and 2 cups bread flour bread flour to the yeast mixture. Stir until mixture is thick and smoothly blended.

Gradually, ¼ cup at a time, add about 1 more cup of bread flour to the mixture. Continue stirring after each addition of flour. This is important in forming the dough. When the dough sticks together and pulls cleanly away from the sides of the bowl, stop adding flour.

4. PREHEATING

When you turn the oven on to preheat it, place an oven thermometer in the center of the middle shelf of the oven.

After 20 minutes, read the oven thermometer. You may need to adjust the temperature. Many ovens do not bake at the temperature the dial indicates. Check your oven temperature once every 6 months.

Preheat the oven to 350 degrees. The oven needs to preheat for 20 minutes.

5. KNEADING

Measure 1 more cup bread flour for kneading and shaping.

Lightly flour the work surface. Place the dough on the work surface. Lightly flour the dough.

Fold the dough in half.

Using the heels of your hands, push the dough down and away from you with a rolling motion.

Turn the dough a quarter turn.

Repeat this sequence of folding, pushing and turning for 5 minutes, until the dough is smooth, elastic and easy to handle. The dough will get firmer as you knead.

As you knead, continue to lightly flour the work surface and the dough with flour so the dough does not get sticky.

Knead gently so that you stretch the dough, but do not tear open the smooth surface of the dough.

If dry clumps of flour stick to your hands, wash and dry your hands. Your hands and the work surface should be smooth to knead and shape the dough.

Do not try to mix lumps of dry dough from the bowl or work surface into the dough. They will not blend in.

6. SHAPING

Place the dough to the side and scrape the work surface clean with a metal spatula or dough scraper before shaping.

Take the time to shape the rolls nicely. Beautiful bread that tastes good is a work of art.

Shape the dough into a ball. Use the smoothest part of the dough as the outside of the ball. Without tearing the outside surface of the dough, stretch and tuck the dough under to form a ball. Let the ball rest on the work surface for 3 minutes.

Using your hand and a rolling pin, pat and roll the first ball out into a 15x9-inch rectangle.

The exact size does not matter.

Filling

Spread 1 tablespoon melted butter on the rectangle.

In a small bowl, mix ½ cup granulated sugar with 1½ teaspoons of cinnamon.

Sprinkle the cinnamon mixture on top of the butter.

Beginning with the 9-inch side nearest you, roll the dough up tightly, jellyroll style away from you. Pinch the last of the roll firmly to the rolled up dough.

Using the serrated bread knife and a sawing motion, cut into 12 rolls.

Place the rolls on the baking sheet with the spiral part of the rolls facing up. Leave space between the rolls.

7. RISING

Let the rolls rise until they double in size, a process that usually takes about 10 to 15 minutes.

8. BAKING

Place the baking sheet in the center of the oven shelf. This shelf should be in the middle of the oven.

On the oven shelf, leave space all the way around the baking sheet to allow the heat to circulate.

Do not open the oven during the first 10 minutes of baking because the dough is completing the rising process.

Some ovens are warmer in the back, front or on one side. Halfway through the baking time, rotate the baking sheet.

Check the rolls 5 minutes before the suggested minimal baking time.

Bake the rolls for 18 to 22 minutes or until golden-brown on the tops and bottoms. Do not over bake.

9. COOLING

When the rolls have finished baking, use a spatula to take the rolls off the baking sheet and place them on a wire cooling rack. There must be airspace around the rolls, including the bottoms, so they do not get wet as they cool.

10. GLAZING

In a small bowl, mix together ¾ cup powdered sugar, 1 tablespoon melted butter, 1 tablespoon soft cream cheese, 1 teaspoon vanilla flavoring and 1 to 2 tablespoons milk. Stir until well blended. The mixture should be thick, but still runny. Add more milk if necessary.

Drizzle over warm rolls. Rolls can be eaten warm.

11. THANKING, EATING, SHARING

Give thanks. Eat some. Share some.

12. RECORDING WHAT YOU HAVE LEARNED

Write notes on the recipe about the amount of bread flour you used, the rising time, the baking temperature, the baking time and any changes you may have made to the recipe.

13. STORING

The rolls must cool for about 1½ hours before storing them.

Store on paper plates in gallon size plastic zipper bags.

14. FREEZING

Rolls that you are not going to eat in the first 2 days should be kept in the freezer.

Store the rolls on paper plates in gallon size plastic freezer zipper bags. They are thicker than the regular zipper bags.

Try to get the air out of the bags before closing them.

Write the date on the bags with a permanent marker. Rolls can be kept in the freezer for 3 months.

15. DEFROSTING

Defrost the bread by taking it out of the zipper bags.

Brush off any ice crystals.

You can defrost the rolls at room temperature on a wire cooling rack.

16. MAKING THIS RECIPE AGAIN

In a couple of days, make this recipe again. Each time it will turn out even better.

CINNAMON/RAISIN ROLLS

Sprinkle cinnamon mixture on top of the melted butter.

Sprinkle 1 cup of soft raisins over the cinnamon mixture, before rolling up the dough.

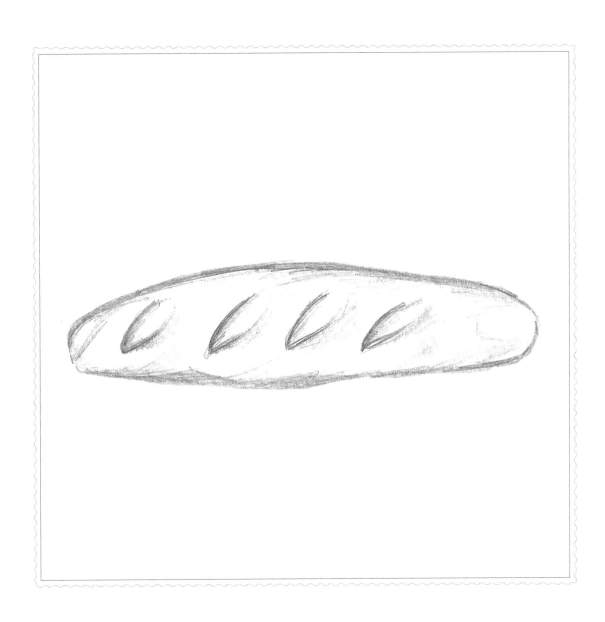

FRENCH STYLE BREAD AND ROLLS

SEMOLINA FRENCH BREAD

People love French bread. It is made with very simple ingredients and is a slightly salty, firm bread with a chewy crust. It makes excellent garlic toast.

YIELD

1 long loaf or 6 large rolls or 8 medium rolls

1. CHECK YOUR YEAST

If you store your yeast in an airtight container in the refrigerator, write the expiration date of the yeast on the container with a permanent marker. Use the yeast before the expiration date.

If you are unsure of the expiration date of the yeast, in a small bowl measure 1 cup warm water, 1 tablespoon yeast and 1 tablespoon sugar. Stir until the yeast and sugar dissolve.

Allow the mixture to sit for 10 minutes. If the mixture does not bubble, you must get new yeast before making the bread.

INGREDIENTS YOU WILL NEED FOR SEMOLINA FRENCH BREAD

1½ cups warm water
1 tablespoon instant yeast
1 tablespoon honey
1½ level teaspoons salt
½ cup semolina flour
2½ to 3½ cups bread flour
3 to 4 tablespoons of corn meal for sprinkling the baking pan

Glaze

Water in a spray bottle or 1 egg white beaten with 1 tablespoon water

Topping

¼ teaspoon coarse salt

2. GETTING READY

As you stay focused on making the bread, your mind will quiet. Enjoy the peacefulness.

Read the entire recipe.

Gather all the equipment and ingredients necessary to make the bread.

Clean a counter space or a tabletop to work.

Spray a 16½x11½-inch heavy-duty aluminum-baking sheet with canola cooking spray. Sprinkle the pan with cornmeal.

3. MEASURING AND STIRRING

Use a large spoon for stirring and measuring.

Pour 1½ cups warm water into a large mixing bowl. Sprinkle 1 tablespoon yeast over the water. Stir until the yeast dissolves.

Add 1 tablespoon honey to the yeast mixture. Stir until well blended.

Flour

Keep the bread flour in a large metal or plastic container. Before measuring the flour, sift through the flour several times in the flour container with the large spoon. If the flour is packed together, you will get too much flour in each cup.

With the large spoon, scoop the flour into the measuring cup until it is overflowing. This takes about 3 to 4 spoonfuls to do.

With the straight side of a dinner knife, remove the excess flour so that the flour is level with the top of the cup.

Spoon the semolina flour into the measuring cup using a smaller spoon.

Add 1½ level teaspoons of salt, ½ cup semolina flour and 1½ cups bread flour to the yeast mixture. Stir until mixture is thick and smoothly blended.

Gradually, ¼ cup at a time, add up to 1 more cup of bread flour to the mixture. Continue stirring after each addition of flour. This is important in forming the dough. When the dough sticks together and pulls cleanly away from the sides of the bowl, stop adding flour.

4. PREHEATING

When you turn the oven on to preheat it, place an oven thermometer in the center of the middle shelf of the oven.

After 20 minutes, read the oven thermometer. You may need to adjust the temperature. Many ovens do not bake at the temperature the dial indicates. Check your oven temperature once every 6 months.

Preheat the oven to 400 degrees. The oven needs to preheat for 20 minutes.

5. KNEADING

Measure 1 more cup bread flour for kneading and shaping.

Lightly flour the work surface. Place the dough on the work surface. Lightly flour the dough.

Fold the dough in half.

Using the heels of your hands, push the dough down and away from you with a rolling motion.

Turn the dough a quarter turn.

Repeat this sequence of folding, pushing and turning for 5 minutes, until the dough is smooth, elastic and easy to handle. The dough will get firmer as you knead.

As you knead, continue to lightly flour the work surface and the dough with flour so the dough does not get sticky.

Knead gently so that you stretch the dough, but do not tear open the smooth surface of the dough.

If dry clumps of flour stick to your hands, wash and dry your hands. Your hands and the work surface should be smooth to knead and shape the dough.

Do not try to mix lumps of dry dough from the bowl or work surface into the dough. They will not blend in.

6. SHAPING

Place the dough to the side and scrape the work surface clean with a metal spatula or dough scraper before shaping.

Take the time to shape the loaves or rolls nicely. Beautiful bread that tastes good is a work of art.

If you are making a loaf, shape the dough into a ball, using the smoothest part of the dough as the outside of the ball. Without tearing the outside surface of the dough, stretch and tuck the dough under to form a ball.

Let the ball rest on the work surface for 3 minutes.

To form the loaf, place the smoothest side of the ball as the outside surface. With your hands, pat the ball into a rectangle, about 12x8-inches. The exact size does not matter.

Starting with the 8-inch side nearest you, firmly, but without tearing the outer surface of the dough, roll the dough away from you into a log.

Pinch the seam together and push into the dough. Push in and tuck under the two ends of the dough. Place the loaf seam side down on the baking sheet.

If you are making rolls, lightly flour the work surface and place the dough on the work surface. Lightly flour the dough.

Cut the dough into 6 to 8 pieces.

To make rolls, use the smoothest part of the dough as the outside of the roll. Without tearing the outside surface of the dough, stretch and tuck the dough under to form a ball.

Place on the baking sheet.

Repeat with each piece of dough. Leave space between the rolls.

7. RISING

Let the loaf rise until it *almost* doubles in size. Usually this takes about 10 to 15 minutes. Instant yeast raises the dough in half the time of regular yeast.

Let the rolls rise until they double in size. Usually this takes about 10 to 15 minutes. Instant yeast raises the dough in half the time of regular yeast.

8. SLASHING

Using a sharp knife, **slash the top of the loaf** with 4 diagonal slashes, about ¼ inch deep.

Slash the top of the rolls with 2 diagonal slashes, about ¼ inch deep.

9. GLAZING

Spray water on the top crust with a spray bottle or brush 1 egg white beaten with 1 tablespoon water on top of crust.

10. TOPPING

¼ teaspoon coarse salt

11. BAKING

Place the baking sheet in the center of the middle shelf of the oven.

On the oven shelf, leave space all the way around the baking sheet to allow the heat to circulate.

Do not open the oven during the first 10 minutes of baking because the dough is completing the rising process.

Some ovens are warmer in the back, front or on one side. Halfway through the baking time, rotate the baking sheet.

Check the loaf and rolls 5 minutes before the suggested minimal baking time.

Bake the loaf for 30 to 35 minutes or until golden-brown on the top, sides and bottom. Do not over bake.

Bake the rolls for 15 to 18 minutes or until golden-brown on the tops and bottoms. Do not over bake.

12. COOLING

If you are making a loaf, immediately remove the loaf from the baking sheet and cool on a wire cooling rack. There must be air space around the loaf, including the bottom, so it does not get wet as it cools.

Cool for 20 minutes before cutting. As the loaf cools, it is actually still cooking and completing the baking process.

If you are making rolls, use a spatula to take the rolls off the baking sheet and place them on a wire cooling rack. There must be air space around the rolls, including the bottoms, so they do not get wet as they cool. Rolls can be eaten warm.

When the bread is cool, slice it on a cutting board with a serrated knife. Use a sawing motion as you cut, so you do not squash the bread.

13. THANKING, EATING, SHARING

Give thanks. Eat some. Share some.

14. RECORDING WHAT YOU HAVE LEARNED

Write notes on the recipe about the amount of bread flour you used, the rising time, the baking temperature, the baking time and any changes you may have made to the recipe.

15. STORING

Bread must cool for about 1½ hours before storing it.

Store bread in gallon size plastic zipper bags.

16. FREEZING

Bread that you are not going to eat in the first 2 days should be kept in the freezer.

Store bread in gallon size plastic freezer zipper bags. They are thicker than the regular zipper bags.

Try to get the air out of the bags before closing them.

Write the date on the bags with a permanent marker. Bread can be kept in the freezer for 3 months.

17. DEFROSTING

Defrost the bread by taking it out of the zipper bags.

Brush off any ice crystals.

You can defrost the bread at room temperature on a wire cooling rack.

Sliced bread can be put in a toaster to defrost it.

18. MAKING THIS RECIPE AGAIN

In a couple of days, make this recipe again. Each time it will turn out even better.

PRETZELS

Of all the bread I have ever made, pretzels are the all-time favorite. This recipe makes a firm, chewy pretzel that is very filling and has no oil. They are good cut in half horizontally and toasted. They can be used for sandwiches. The dough can be formed into shapes such as letters, numbers, animals, hearts, etc. This is a fun baking activity for kids.

YIELD

6 large pretzels or 8 medium sized pretzels

1. CHECK YOUR YEAST

If you store your yeast in an airtight container in the refrigerator, write the expiration date of the yeast on the container with a permanent marker. Use the yeast before the expiration date.

If you are unsure of the expiration date of the yeast, in a small bowl measure 1 cup warm water, 1 tablespoon yeast and 1 tablespoon sugar. Stir until the yeast and sugar dissolve.

Allow the mixture to sit for 10 minutes. If the mixture does not bubble, you must get new yeast before making the bread.

INGREDIENTS YOU WILL NEED FOR PRETZELS

1½ cups warm water
1 tablespoon instant yeast
1 tablespoon honey
1½ level teaspoons salt
½ cup semolina flour
2½ to 3½ cups bread flour
3 to 4 tablespoons of cornmeal

Glaze

1 beaten egg

Topping

½ teaspoon coarse salt or Parmesan cheese that comes in a plastic canister (Sprinkle the cheese from the canister.)

2. GETTING READY

As you stay focused on making the bread, your mind will quiet. Enjoy the peacefulness.

Read the entire recipe.

Gather all the equipment and ingredients necessary to make the bread.

Clean a counter space or a tabletop to work on.

Spray a 16½x11½-inch heavy-duty aluminum-baking sheet with canola cooking spray. Sprinkle the pan with cornmeal.

3. MEASURING AND STIRRING

Use a large spoon for stirring and measuring.

Pour 1½ cups warm water into a large mixing bowl. Sprinkle 1 tablespoon yeast over the water. Stir until the yeast dissolves.

Add 1 tablespoon honey to the yeast mixture. Stir until well blended.

Flour

Keep the bread flour in a large metal or plastic container. Before measuring the flour, sift through the flour several times in the flour container with the large spoon. If the flour is packed together, you will get too much flour in each cup.

With the large spoon, scoop the flour into the measuring cup until it is overflowing. This takes about 3 to 4 spoonfuls to do.

With the straight side of a dinner knife, remove the excess flour so that the flour is level with the top of the cup.

Spoon the semolina flour into the measuring cup with a smaller spoon.

Add 1½ level teaspoons of salt, ½ cup semolina flour and 1½ cups bread flour to the yeast mixture. Stir until mixture is thick and smoothly blended.

Gradually, ¼ cup at a time, add up to 1 more cup of bread flour to the mixture. Continue stirring after each addition of flour. This is important in forming the dough. When the dough sticks together and pulls cleanly away from the sides of the bowl, stop adding flour.

4. PREHEATING

When you turn the oven on to preheat it, place an oven thermometer in the center of the middle shelf of the oven.

After 20 minutes, read the oven thermometer. You may need to adjust the temperature. Many ovens do not bake at the temperature the dial indicates. Check your oven temperature once every 6 months.

Preheat the oven to 425 degrees. The oven needs to preheat for 20 minutes.

5. KNEADING

Measure 1 more cup bread flour for kneading and shaping.

Lightly flour the work surface. Place the dough on the work surface. Lightly flour the dough.

Fold the dough in half.

Using the heels of your hands, push the dough down and away from you with a rolling motion.

Turn the dough a quarter turn.

Repeat this sequence of folding, pushing and turning for 5 minutes, until the dough is smooth, elastic and easy to handle. The dough will get firmer as you knead.

As you knead, continue to lightly flour the work surface and the dough with flour so the dough does not get sticky.

Knead gently so that you stretch the dough, but do not tear open the smooth surface of the dough.

If dry clumps of flour stick to your hands, wash and dry your hands. Your hands and the work surface should be smooth to knead and shape the dough.

Do not try to mix lumps of dry dough from the bowl or work surface into the dough. They will not blend in.

6. SHAPING

Place the dough to the side and scrape the work surface clean with a metal spatula or dough scraper before shaping.

Take the time to shape the pretzels nicely. Beautiful bread that tastes good is a work of art.

Cut the dough into 6 to 8 pieces.

Shape each piece into a ball. Use the smoothest part of the dough as the outside of the ball. Without tearing the outside surface of the dough stretch and tuck the dough under to form a ball.

Let the pieces rest for 3 minutes.

Keep the work surface and the dough lightly floured.

Choose the smoothest part of the dough as the outside. Roll one piece of dough at a time into a 16-inch rope and form it into the pretzel shape as shown in the drawings. If the work surface is too slippery, brush the flour to the side, lightly spray the work surface with a little canola cooking spray and lightly flour it again. The dough should adhere a little to the work surface, but not stick to it.

Place pretzels on the baking sheet, leaving space between pretzels.

7. GLAZING

Brush the tops of the pretzels with the beaten egg.

8. TOPPING

Sprinkle on ½ teaspoon coarse salt or sprinkle liberally with Parmesan cheese.

No Rising

Pretzels **do not rise** before putting them in the oven.

9. BAKING

Place the baking sheet in the center of the middle shelf of the oven.

On the oven shelf, leave space all the way around the baking sheet to allow the heat to circulate.

Do not open the oven during the first 10 minutes of baking because the dough is completing the rising process.

Some ovens are warmer in the back, front or on one side. Halfway through the baking time, rotate the baking sheet.

Check the pretzels 5 minutes before the suggested minimal baking time.

Bake the pretzels for 18 to 22 minutes or until golden-brown on the tops and bottoms. Do not over bake.

10. COOLING

When the pretzels have finished baking, use a spatula to take them off the baking sheet and place them on a wire cooling rack. There must be air space around the pretzels, including the bottoms, so they do not get wet as they cool.

Allow the pretzels to cool for at least 5 minutes before eating.

11. THANKING, EATING, SHARING

Give thanks. Eat some. Share some.

12. RECORDING WHAT YOU HAVE LEARNED

Write notes on the recipe about the amount of bread flour you used, the rising time, the baking temperature, the baking time and any changes you may have made to the recipe.

13. STORING

Pretzels must cool about an hour before storing them.

Pretzels should be stored in a paper or cloth bag, rather than a plastic bag.

14. FREEZING

Pretzels get stale quickly because there is no oil in them. Whatever will not be eaten in the first two days should be stored in the freezer.

Store pretzels in gallon size plastic freezer zipper bags. They are thicker than the regular zipper bags.

Try to get the air out of the bags before closing them.

Write the date on the bags with a permanent marker. Pretzels can be kept in the freezer for 3 months.

15. DEFROSTING

Defrost the pretzels by taking them out of the zipper bags.

Brush off any ice crystals.

You can defrost the pretzels at room temperature on a wire cooling rack.

16. MAKING THIS RECIPE AGAIN

In a couple of days, make this recipe again. Each time it will turn out even better.

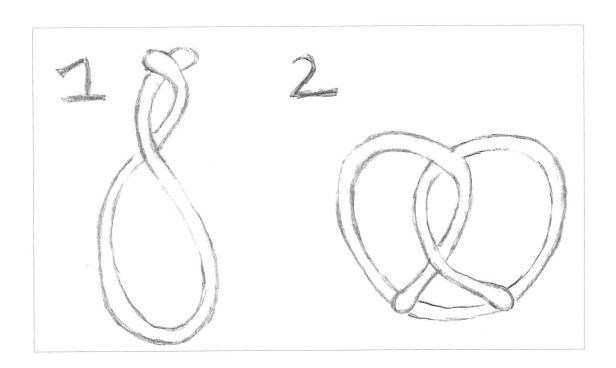

BREADSTICKS

Delicious and simple to make.

YIELD

8 breadsticks

1. CHECK YOUR YEAST

If you store your yeast in an airtight container in the refrigerator, write the expiration date of the yeast on the container with a permanent marker. Use the yeast before the expiration date.

If you are unsure of the expiration date of the yeast, in a small bowl measure 1 cup warm water, 1 tablespoon yeast and 1 tablespoon sugar. Stir until the yeast and sugar dissolve.

Allow the mixture to sit for 10 minutes. If the mixture does not bubble, you must get new yeast before making the bread.

INGREDIENTS YOU WILL NEED FOR BREADSTICKS

1½ cups warm water
1 tablespoon instant yeast
1 tablespoon brown sugar
1½ level teaspoons salt
½ cup semolina flour
2½ to 3½ cups bread flour
3 to 4 tablespoons of cornmeal

Glaze

1 beaten egg

Topping

½ teaspoon coarse salt or Parmesan cheese that comes in a plastic canister (Sprinkle the cheese from the canister.) or 1 tablespoon poppy seeds or 1 tablespoon sesame seeds

2. GETTING READY

As you stay focused on making the bread, your mind will quiet. Enjoy the peacefulness.

Read the entire recipe.

Gather all the equipment and ingredients necessary to make the bread.

Clean a counter space or a tabletop to work on.

Spray a 16½x11½-inch heavy-duty aluminum-baking sheet with canola cooking spray. Sprinkle the pan with cornmeal.

3. MEASURING AND STIRRING

Use a large spoon for stirring and measuring.

Pour 1½ cups warm water into a large mixing bowl. Sprinkle 1 tablespoon yeast over the water. Stir until the yeast dissolves.

Add 1 tablespoon brown sugar to the yeast mixture. Stir until well blended.

Flour

Keep the bread flour in a large metal or plastic container. Before measuring the flour, sift through the flour several times in the flour container with the large spoon. If the flour is packed together, you will get too much flour in each cup.

With the large spoon, scoop the flour into the measuring cup until it is overflowing. This takes about 3 to 4 spoonfuls to do.

With the straight side of a dinner knife, remove the excess flour so that the flour is level with the top of the cup.

Spoon the semolina flour into the measuring cup with a smaller spoon.

Add 1½ level teaspoons of salt, ½ cup semolina flour and 1½ cups bread flour to the yeast mixture. Stir until mixture is thick and smoothly blended.

Gradually, ¼ cup at a time, add up to 1 more cup of bread flour to the mixture. Continue stirring after each addition of flour. This is important in forming the dough. When the dough sticks together and pulls cleanly away from the sides of the bowl, stop adding flour.

4. PREHEATING

When you turn the oven on to preheat it, place an oven thermometer in the center of the middle shelf of the oven.

After 20 minutes, read the oven thermometer. You may need to adjust the temperature. Many ovens do not bake at the temperature the dial indicates.

Check your oven temperature once every 6 months.

Preheat the oven to 425 degrees. The oven needs to preheat for 20 minutes.

5. KNEADING

Measure 1 more cup bread flour for kneading and shaping.

Lightly flour the work surface. Place the dough on the work surface. Lightly flour the dough.

Fold the dough in half.

Using the heels of your hands, push the dough down and away from you with a rolling motion.

Turn the dough a quarter turn.

Repeat this sequence of folding, pushing and turning for 5 minutes, until the dough is smooth, elastic and easy to handle. The dough will get firmer as you knead.

As you knead, continue to lightly flour the work surface and the dough with flour so the dough does not get sticky.

Knead gently so that you stretch the dough, but do not tear open the smooth surface of the dough.

If dry clumps of flour stick to your hands, wash and dry your hands. Your hands and the work surface should be smooth to knead and shape the dough.

Do not try to mix lumps of dry dough from the bowl or work surface into the dough. They will not blend in.

6. SHAPING

Place the dough to the side and scrape the work surface clean with a metal spatula or dough scraper before shaping.

Take the time to shape the breadsticks nicely. Beautiful bread that tastes good is a work of art.

Lightly flour the work surface and place the dough on the work surface. Lightly flour the dough.

Cut the dough into 6 to 8 pieces.

Shape each piece into a ball. Use the smoothest part of the dough as the outside of the ball. Without tearing the outside surface of the dough, stretch and tuck the dough under to form a ball.

Let the pieces rest for 3 minutes.

Keep the work surface and the dough lightly floured.

Roll one piece of dough at a time into a 9-inch rope. If the work surface is too slippery, brush the flour to the side, lightly spray the work surface with a little canola cooking spray and lightly flour the work surface again. The dough should adhere a little to the work surface, but not stick to it.

Place on baking sheet, leaving space between the breadsticks.

7. GLAZING

Brush the tops of the breadsticks with the beaten egg.

8. TOPPING

Sprinkle on ½ teaspoon coarse salt or sprinkle liberally with Parmesan cheese or sprinkle with 1 tablespoon poppy seeds or sprinkle with 1 tablespoon sesame seeds or use any combination of the toppings.

No Rising

Breadsticks **do not rise** before putting them in the oven.

9. BAKING

Place the baking sheet in the center of the middle shelf of the oven.

On the oven shelf, leave space all the way around the baking sheet to allow the heat to circulate.

Do not open the oven during the first 10 minutes of baking because the dough is completing the rising process.

Some ovens are warmer in the back, front or on one side. Halfway through the baking time, rotate the baking sheet.

Check the breadsticks 5 minutes before the suggested minimal baking time.

Bake the breadsticks for 18 to 22 minutes or until golden-brown on the tops and bottoms.

Do not over bake.

10. COOLING

When the breadsticks have finished baking, use a spatula to take them off the baking sheet and place them on a wire cooling rack. There must be air space around the breadsticks, including the bottoms, so they do not get wet as they cool.

Allow the breadsticks to cool for at least 5 minutes before eating.

11. THANKING, EATING, SHARING

Give thanks. Eat some. Share some.

12. RECORDING WHAT YOU HAVE LEARNED

Write notes on the recipe about the amount of bread flour you used, the rising time, the baking temperature, the baking time and any changes you may have made to the recipe.

13. STORING

Breadsticks must cool for about an hour before storing them.

Breadsticks should be stored in a paper bag or a cloth bag, rather than a plastic bag.

14. FREEZING

Breadsticks get stale quickly because there is no oil in them. Whatever will not be eaten in the first two days should be stored in the freezer.

Put breadsticks in gallon size plastic freezer zipper bags. They are thicker than the regular zipper bags.

Try to get the air out of the bags before closing them.

Write the date on the bags with a permanent marker. Breadsticks can be kept in the freezer for 3 months.

15. DEFROSTING

Defrost the breadsticks by taking them out of the zipper bags.

Brush off any ice crystals.

You can defrost the breadsticks at room temperature on a wire cooling rack.

16. MAKING THIS RECIPE AGAIN

In a couple of days, make this recipe again. Each time it will turn out even better.

THINGS THAT CAN GO WRONG WITH BREAD AND HOW TO FIX THEM

The dough did not rise.
- The yeast may no longer be active. Test your yeast. If it does not bubble, get new yeast.
- Was the water too hot that you dissolved the yeast in? If the water is too hot, it kills the yeast. Use warm water.
- Be sure that at least half of the flour used was some form of wheat flour.

The bread fell instead of rose in the oven.
- The dough may have risen too high before you put it in the oven.

The free form bread did not hold its shape and is rather flat.
- The dough was too soft to hold its shape. It needed more flour.

The bread baked unevenly.
- Some ovens are warmer in the back, front or on one side. Halfway through the baking time, rotate the loaf pans or baking sheet.

The crust is too pale.
- The oven temperature was not high enough.
- The bread did not bake long enough.

The crust is too dark.
- The bread baked too long.
- The oven temperature was too high.
- Place the baking sheet in the center of the oven shelf. This shelf should be in the middle of the oven.

The bread is too heavy.
- Use less flour.
- Use less whole-wheat flour and more bread flour.

The center of the bread is still raw.
- The bread needed to cook longer.
- Try cooking the bread 25 degrees higher next time.

The dough is too dry.
- Bake for less time.

The bread has lines of flour in it.
- The dough was not kneaded thoroughly.

The flavor isn't good.
- Did you forget to add the salt?

The bread is too salty.
- Add less salt.

The bread is too sweet.
- Add less sweetener.

INVENT YOUR OWN RECIPES

As you become more experienced, be creative. Breadmaking is a very flexible art. You can use a different liquid, vary the amount of sweetener, use a different sweetener or not use a sweetener. You can add less salt or omit the salt. You can use a different fat. You can try different flours and combinations of flour. You can add extra ingredients to the recipe, such as cheese, vegetables, dried fruits, nuts, spices, seasonings, herbs, etc. You can experiment with various glazes.

You can use any combinations of flour you like, but at least half of the flour in any yeast bread must be bread flour, unbleached all-purpose flour or whole-wheat flour. Bread flour and unbleached all-purpose flour can be used interchangeably. You can add rye flour, rice flour, soy flour, cornmeal, raw oatmeal, oat flour, oat bran, wheat germ, mashed potato flakes, cooked cereal, etc., to any recipe.

Make bread to suit your taste and heath needs. Have fun!

CONVERTING OTHER RECIPES TO THIS SIMPLE WAY

You can take almost any recipe you find, except for artisan and sourdough bread, and make it in this same easy way.

1. Dissolve the instant yeast in warm water. Be sure the yeast is still active.

2. Add the sweetener and all the liquid ingredients to the yeast mixture. Allow any hot ingredients to cool first, before adding them to the yeast mixture. Warm any cold ingredients, before adding them to the yeast mixture. Stir.

3. Add the salt and about ⅓ of the flour. Stir until the mixture is thick and smooth.

4. Add enough flour, so the dough pulls cleanly away from the sides of the bowl.

5. Measure 1 more cup of flour to knead and shape the dough. Knead the dough for 5 minutes.

6. Shape the dough.

7. Let the dough rise. There is no first rising of the dough before shaping it.

8. Bake the dough.

9. Let the bread cool.

10. Slice if necessary.

11. Give thanks. Eat some. Share some.

MUFFINS

BLUEBERRY MUFFINS

These delicious muffins are loaded with berries.
Blueberries add fiber and important nutrients.

YIELD

12 standard size muffins

INGREDIENTS YOU WILL NEED FOR BLUEBERRY MUFFINS

Unbleached Flour

Use unbleached all-purpose flour, instead of bread flour. The high gluten content in the bread flour will make the muffins tough. Unbleached all-purpose flour has less gluten.

Dry Ingredients

1 cup unbleached all-purpose flour
¾ cup whole-wheat flour
½ cup brown sugar
2 teaspoons baking powder
¼ level teaspoon salt
1½ cups fresh or frozen blueberries

Wet ingredients

1 egg
¼ cup canola oil
1 cup milk

1. GETTING READY

As you stay focused on making the muffins, your mind will quiet. Enjoy the peacefulness.

Read the entire recipe.

Gather all the equipment and ingredients necessary to make the muffins.

Clean off a counter space or a tabletop to work on.

2. PREHEATING

When you turn the oven on to preheat it, place an oven thermometer in the middle of the middle rack of the oven.

After 20 minutes, read the oven thermometer. You may need to adjust the temperature. Many ovens do not bake at the temperature the dial indicates. Check your oven temperature once every 6 months.

Preheat oven to 350 degrees.

Line muffin cups with foil liners or spray them with canola vegetable cooking spray.

3. MEASURING AND STIRRING

Use a large spoon for stirring and measuring.

Flour

Keep the unbleached all-purpose flour and whole-wheat flour in large metal or plastic containers.

Before measuring the flour, sift through the flour several times in the flour container with a large spoon. If the flour is packed together, you will get too much flour in each cup.

Use a large spoon to scoop the unbleached all-purpose flour into the measuring cup, until it is overflowing. This takes about 3 to 4 spoonfuls to do.

Then with the straight side of a dinner knife, remove the excess flour so that the flour is level with the top of the cup.

Spoon the whole-wheat flour into the measuring cup with a smaller spoon.

In a medium size bowl, mix together until evenly blended, 1 cup unbleached all-purpose flour, ¾ cup whole-wheat flour, ½ cup brown sugar, 2 teaspoons baking powder and ¼ level teaspoon salt. I like to use my hands to do this. Add 1½ cups blueberries. Stir with a spoon.

In another medium size bowl, combine 1 egg, ¼ cup canola oil and 1 cup milk. Beat together with a whisk or a fork, until well blended.

Make a well by pushing the dry ingredients up around the sides of the bowl with a spoon.

Pour the wet ingredients into the center of the well.

Gently fold the dry ingredients into the wet ones, until all the dry ingredients are moistened. Use only about 15 strokes. The batter may be lumpy. Do not over mix.

4. PUTTING THE BATTER INTO THE MUFFIN CUPS

Using a ¼ cup measuring cup to scoop and pour the batter, fill the muffin cups two-thirds full.

5. BAKING

Place the muffin tin in the center of the middle shelf of the oven.

On the oven shelf, leave space all the way around the muffin tin to allow the heat to circulate.

Some ovens are warmer in the back, front or on one side. Halfway through the baking time, rotate the muffin tin.

Check the muffins 5 minutes before the suggested minimal baking time.

Bake the muffins for 20 to 22 minutes. Muffins are done when the tops are lightly browned and the centers are firm to the touch. Do not over bake the muffins or they will be hard.

6. COOLING

While still in the muffin tin, let the muffins cool for 10 minutes on the wire cooling rack.

Then remove the muffins from the muffin tin and place them on the wire cooling rack to continue cooling.

7. THANKING, EATING, SHARING

Muffins are best served fresh and still slightly warm.

Give thanks. Eat some. Share some.

8. RECORDING WHAT YOU HAVE LEARNED

Write notes on any changes you may have made to the recipe.

9. STORING

Muffins must cool for about an hour before storing them.

Store muffins in a gallon size plastic zipper bags.

10. FREEZING

Muffins that you are not going to use within the first 2 days should be frozen.

Put muffins in gallon size plastic freezer zipper bags. They are thicker than the regular zipper bags.

Try to get the air out of the bags before closing them.

Write the date on the bags with a permanent marker. Muffins can be kept in the freezer for 3 months.

11. DEFROSTING

Defrost the muffins by taking them out of the zipper bags.

Brush off any ice particles.

Place on a wire cooling rack and allow muffins to defrost at room temperature.

12 MAKING THIS RECIPE AGAIN

In a couple of days, make this recipe again. Each time it will turn out even better.

PUMPKIN MUFFINS

Moist, delicious, filling.

YIELD

12 standard size muffins

INGREDIENTS YOU WILL NEED FOR PUMPKIN MUFFINS

Unbleached Flour

Use unbleached all-purpose flour, instead of bread flour. The high gluten content in the bread flour will make the muffins tough. Unbleached all-purpose flour has less gluten.

Dry ingredients

1 cup unbleached all-purpose flour
1 cup whole-wheat flour
½ cup brown sugar
2 teaspoons baking powder
¼ level teaspoon salt
1½ teaspoons pumpkin pie spice
1 cup dates

Wet ingredients

1 cup canned pumpkin
1 egg
¼ cup canola oil
¾ cup milk

1. GETTING READY

As you stay focused on making the muffins, your mind will quiet. Enjoy the peacefulness.

Read the entire recipe.

Gather all the equipment and ingredients necessary to make the muffins.

Clean off a counter space or a tabletop to work on.

2. PREHEATING

When you turn the oven on to preheat it, place an oven thermometer in the middle of the middle rack of the oven.

After 20 minutes, read the oven thermometer. You may need to adjust the temperature. Many ovens do not bake at the temperature the dial indicates. Check your oven temperature once every 6 months.

Preheat oven to 350 degrees.

Line muffin cups with foil liners or spray them with canola vegetable cooking spray.

3. MEASURING AND STIRRING

Use a large spoon for stirring and measuring.

Flour

Keep the unbleached all-purpose flour and whole-wheat flour in large metal or plastic containers.

Before measuring the flour, sift through the flour several times in the flour container with a large spoon. If the flour is packed together, you will get too much flour in each cup.

Use a large spoon to scoop the flour into the measuring cup, until it is overflowing. This takes about 3 to 4 spoonfuls to do.

Then with the straight side of a dinner knife, remove the excess flour so that the flour is level with the top of the cup.

In a medium size bowl, mix together until evenly blended, 1 cup unbleached all-purpose flour, 1 cup whole-wheat flour, ½ cup brown sugar, 2 teaspoons baking powder, ¼ level teaspoon salt and 1½ teaspoons pumpkin pie spice. I like to use my hands to do this. Add 1 cup dates. Stir with a spoon.

In another medium size bowl, combine 1 cup canned pumpkin, 1 egg, ¼ cup canola oil and ¾ cup milk. Beat together with a whisk or fork, until well blended.

Make a well by pushing the dry ingredients up around the sides of the bowl with a spoon.

Pour the wet ingredients into the center of the well.

Gently fold the dry ingredients into the wet ones, until all the dry ingredients are moistened. Use only about 15 strokes. The batter may be lumpy. Do not over mix.

4. PUTTING THE BATTER INTO THE MUFFIN CUPS

Using a ¼ cup measuring cup to scoop and pour the batter, fill the muffin cups two-thirds full.

5. BAKING

Place the muffin tin in the center of the middle shelf of the oven.

On the oven shelf, leave space all the way around the muffin tin to allow the heat to circulate.

Some ovens are warmer in the back, front or on one side. Halfway through the baking time, rotate the muffin tin.

Check the muffins 5 minutes before the suggested minimal baking time.

Bake the muffins for 20 to 22 minutes. Muffins are done when the tops are lightly browned and the centers are firm to the touch. Do not over bake the muffins or they will be hard.

6. COOLING

While still in the muffin tin, let the muffins cool for 5 minutes on the wire cooling rack.

Then remove the muffins from the muffin tin and place them on the wire cooling rack to continue cooling.

7. THANKING, EATING, SHARING

Muffins are best served fresh and still slightly warm.

Give thanks. Eat some. Share some.

8. RECORDING WHAT YOU HAVE LEARNED

Write notes on any changes you may have made to the recipe.

9. STORING

Muffins must cool for about an hour before storing them.

Store muffins in a gallon size plastic zipper bags.

10. FREEZING

Muffins that you are not going to use within the first 2 days should be frozen.

Put muffins in gallon size plastic freezer zipper bags. They are thicker than the regular zipper bags.

Try to get the air out of the bags before closing them.

Write the date on the bags with a permanent marker. Muffins can be kept in the freezer for 3 months.

11. DEFROSTING

Defrost the muffins by taking them out of the zipper bags.

Brush off any ice particles.

Place on a wire cooling rack and allow muffins to defrost at room temperature.

12. MAKING THIS RECIPE AGAIN

In a couple of days, make this recipe again. Each time it will turn out even better.

BRAN MUFFINS

A good source of fiber, a good breakfast muffin.

YIELD

12 standard size muffins

INGREDIENTS YOU WILL NEED FOR BRAN MUFFINS

Dry Ingredients

1½ cups whole-wheat flour
½ cup wheat bran
½ cup brown sugar
2 teaspoons baking powder
¼ level teaspoon salt
½ cup grated carrots
½ cup soft raisins

Wet Ingredients

1 egg
¼ cup canola oil
1 cup milk

1. GETTING READY

As you stay focused on making the muffins, your mind will quiet. Enjoy the peacefulness.

Read the entire recipe.

Gather all the equipment and ingredients necessary to make the muffins.

Clean off a counter space or a tabletop to work on.

2. PREHEATING

When you turn the oven on to preheat it, place an oven thermometer in the middle of the middle rack of the oven.

After 20 minutes, read the oven thermometer. You may need to adjust the temperature. Many ovens do not bake at the temperature the dial indicates. Check your oven temperature once every 6 months.

Preheat oven to 350 degrecs.

Line muffin cups with foil liners or spray them with canola vegetable cooking spray.

3. MEASURING AND STIRRING

Use a large spoon for stirring and measuring.

Flour

Keep the whole-wheat flour in a large metal or plastic container.

Before measuring the flour, sift through the flour several times in the flour container with a large spoon. If the flour is packed together, you will get too much flour in each cup.

Use a large spoon to scoop the flour into the measuring cup, until it is overflowing. This takes about 3 to 4 spoonfuls to do.

Then with the straight side of a dinner knife, remove the excess flour so that the flour is level with the top of the cup.

Spoon the wheat bran into the measuring cup, using a smaller spoon.

In a medium size bowl, mix together until evenly blended, 1½ cups whole-wheat flour, ½ cup wheat bran, ½ cup brown sugar, 2 teaspoons baking powder and ¼ level teaspoon salt. I like to use my hands to do this. Add ½ cup grated carrots and ½ cup soft raisins. Stir with a spoon.

In another medium size bowl, combine 1 egg, ¼ canola oil and 1 cup milk. Beat together with a whisk or a fork, until well blended.

Make a well by pushing the dry ingredients up around the sides of the bowl with a spoon.

Pour the wet ingredients into the center of the well.

Gently fold the dry ingredients into the wet ones, until all the dry ingredients are moistened. Use only about 15 strokes. The batter may be lumpy. Do not over mix.

4. PUTTING THE BATTER INTO THE MUFFIN CUPS

Using a ¼ cup measuring cup to scoop and pour the batter, fill the muffin cups two-thirds full.

5. BAKING

Place the muffin tin in the center of the middle shelf of the oven..

On the oven shelf, leave space all the way around the muffin tin to allow the heat to circulate.

Some ovens are warmer in the back, front or on one side. Halfway through the baking time, rotate the muffin tin.

Check the muffins 5 minutes before the suggested minimal baking time.

Bake the muffins for 20 to 22 minutes. Muffins are done when the tops are lightly browned and the centers are firm to the touch. Do not over bake the muffins or they will be hard.

6. COOLING

While still in the muffin tin, let the muffins cool for 5 minutes on the wire cooling rack.

Then remove the muffins from the muffin tin and place them on the wire cooling rack to continue cooling.

7. THANKING, EATING, SHARING

Muffins are best served fresh and suntil slightly warm.

Give thanks. Eat some. Share some.

8. RECORDING WHAT YOU HAVE LEARNED

Write notes on any changes you may have made to the recipe.

9. STORING

Muffins must cool for about an hour before storing them.

Store muffins in a gallon size plastic zipper bags.

10. FREEZING

Muffins that you are not going to use within the first 2 days should be frozen.

Put muffins in gallon size plastic freezer zipper bags. They are thicker than the regular zipper bags.

Try to get the air out of the bags before closing them.

Write the date on the bags with a permanent marker. Muffins can be kept in the freezer for 3 months.

11. DEFROSTING

Defrost the muffins by taking them out of the zipper bags.

Brush off any ice particles.

Place on a wire cooling rack and allow muffins to defrost at room temperature.

12. MAKING THIS RECIPE AGAIN

In a couple of days, make this recipe again. Each time it will turn out even better.

THINGS THAT CAN GO WRONG WITH MUFFINS AND HOW TO FIX THEM

The muffins are tough.
- Did you use bread flour? Bread flour has more gluten in it and will make the muffins tough. Use unbleached all-purpose flour.
- Perhaps you stirred the batter too long. The batter should be gently folded, only until the dry ingredients are mixed with the wet. It is all right to have lumps. Use about 15 folding strokes.

The muffins are too heavy.
- Did you measure the flour correctly as explained in the recipe? Maybe you added too much flour. Try adding ¼ cup less flour.

Parts of the muffin have a bitter taste.
- The baking powder was not distributed evenly in the dry ingredients. Make sure the baking powder is not lumpy in the dry ingredients or you will taste little bits of it.

Thanks for coming on this journey. If you master these recipes, you will make many people full and happy. May God's sweetest blessings be yours and with all those you love.

BIBLIOGRAPHY

Brown, Edward Espe, *The Tassajara Bread Book*. Boston: Shambhala Publications, Inc. 1986.

Casella, Dolores, *A World of Bread*. Port Washington, New York: David White, Inc. 1996.

Hensperger, Beth, *The Bread Bible*. California: Chronicle Books. 1999.

King Arthur flour Company, Inc., *The King Arthur Flour Baker's Companion*. Woodstock, Vermont: The Countryman Press. 2003.

Summers, Kathy, *Healing With Handmade Bread*. Lincoln, Nebraska: iUniverse. 2004.

Kathy Summers is sixty-five years old. She graduated from Brigham Young University with a degree in art education. She is married to a physician. They have nine wonderful children and twenty-four wonderful grandchildren. She has been baking handmade breads almost every day for thirty-nine years. She helps to raise and train therapy dogs and service dogs. She volunteers with her therapy dog Willy at hospitals and in a school reading program. God's love, kids, dogs and bread-making have blessed her life.